I DON'T MEAN TO SMASH YOUR TOMATOES, HONEY!

I DON'T MEAN TO SMASH YOUR TOMATOES, HONEY!

A Glimpse at Life's Perspectives
from A to Z

Dr. BerNadette Lawson-Williams
Tracie K. Thomas

iUniverse, Inc.
New York Lincoln Shanghai

I Don't Mean to Smash Your Tomatoes, Honey!
A Glimpse at Life's Perspectives from A to Z

iUniverse books may be ordered through booksellers or by contacting:

iUniverse
2021 Pine Lake Road, Suite 100
Lincoln, NE 68512
www.iuniverse.com
1-800-Authors (1-800-288-4677)

Because of the dynamic nature of the Internet, any Web addresses or links contained in this book may have changed since publication and may no longer be valid.

The views expressed in this work are solely those of the author and do not necessarily reflect the views of the publisher, and the publisher hereby disclaims any responsibility for them.

ISBN: 978-0-595-43381-0 (pbk)
ISBN: 978-0-595-68226-3 (cloth)
ISBN: 978-0-595-87707-2 (ebk)

Printed in the United States of America

We dedicate this book to our mothers, aunts, grandmothers, great-grandmothers, cousins, sisters, and mentors, all of whom have helped to mold us into confident, self-sufficient, and respectable women. These great women have provided us with powerful examples of success. We know that without their inspiration, this book could not have been possible. We devote each page of this book to these women and to those whose lives we have positively impacted. As we strive to empower our daughters, nieces, cousins, mentees, and readers like you to reach your full potential, we encourage you to embrace and appreciate your womanhood. Remember, the world is a better place because you exist. You possess the power to ignite our nation.

We also dedicate this book to our fathers, husbands, uncles, grandfathers, brothers, fiancés, boyfriends, ex-boyfriends, and ex-husbands. We are sincerely thankful to you for the life experiences that you have granted us, along with the lessons we have learned from these experiences. Through these experiences we have become more insightful, more resilient, more versatile, and more influential women. Although this book will only allow you to take a glimpse at the life perspectives of 18 women, we urge you to initiate dialogue with the special women in your life regarding their individual perspectives. We hope this book will enable you to gain insight and a better understanding of the emotional, physical, intellectual, spiritual, and mental desires and necessities of these women.

May this book grant you a literary experience that will encourage you to help all women reach their full potential by embracing, appreciating, and enjoying the power of their womanhood. We also hope every chapter of our book will inspire you to share with your daughters, granddaughters, cousins, and nieces that they are capable of achieving any goal that they envision. Finally, we hope that you will emphasize to your sons, grandsons, nephews, and mentees, the importance of appreciating, honoring, and respecting all women. Through these sincere conversations between generations past, present, and future, we can begin paving a path for women and men to live together, love together, and work together, so together we can build a better world!

Contents

EDITORS' NOTE

In the summer of 1999, a mere conversation between two girlfriends ignited the idea of writing a book about the life experiences of young professional women. In October of 2003, the vision of this book was revived when a candid conversation between two different girlfriends gave birth to the title of the book, along with the phrase "smashing tomatoes." Four years later, we are now ready to share with you the life stories and life experiences of 16 ambitious women from Generation X, along with three original poems written by two extraordinary poets.

These vivacious and intelligent women represent nine different states (GA, FL, HI, IL, MD, NC, OH, PA, and SC), 16 different cities, and various social backgrounds. They also represent a variety of educational backgrounds and professional occupations in the areas of: academia, accounting, agribusiness, biology, engineering, entrepreneurship, graphic design, healthcare, history, human services, management, mathematics, nursing, nutrition, pharmaceutical sales, physical education, politics, real estate, social services, speech pathology, sport management, and technology. Most of these women possess advanced degrees and serve as positive role models in their respective communities.

Despite their unique qualities, the co-authors possess many commonalities. Twelve of the co-authors are graduates of South Carolina State

University, two received their graduate degrees from the Ohio State University, nine are members of Delta Sigma Theta Sorority, Incorporated, and three are members of Alpha Kappa Alpha Sorority, Incorporated. Co-author notables include: a New York Marathon runner, a flight attendant, six entrepreneurs, the Principal of Augusta, Georgia's first charter school, two university professors, a recipient of the Who's Who Among America's Teachers Award, and a former Student Ambassador to Russia. Personal interests of these adventurous women include: white-water rafting, playing chess, rock climbing, crocheting, skiing, playing golf, reading, fitness, yoga, sewing, watching sports, shopping, dancing, and traveling worldwide, among many others. Loving wives, mothers, daughters, fiancées, girlfriends, bachelorettes, sisters, nieces, and aunts, these eclectic women represent the diverse perspectives of single, engaged, married, and divorced women everywhere!

The straightforward manner in which the co-authors present their uninhibited opinions, referred to as "smashing tomatoes," offers savvy solutions to the personal and professional issues encountered by many women daily. To ensure that their perspectives are uninhibited and spontaneous, their identities remain anonymous. These women weren't afraid to "smash tomatoes" and we hope that their expressions will motivate you to connect with your inner emotions. Over coffee, tea, or laughs among friends, we wish for you an enjoyable literary journey and encourage you to share this book with the most important people in your life.

LIST OF CONTRIBUTORS

D'Metria Alston

A native of Eutawville, South Carolina, D'Metria received her B.A. degree from South Carolina State University and a M.A. degree in Speech—Language Pathology from The Ohio State University. She is married to her college sweetheart, Anthony. She and Anthony reside in Columbus, Ohio with their three sons: Philip, and twins Timothy and Thomas. D'Metria is a licensed realtor and the owner of Special Occasions by D, a business that specializes in accessories and invitations for all occasions. She enjoys playing golf, shopping, and spending time with her family and friends. D'Metria is a member of Delta Sigma Theta Sorority, Incorporated.

Adrienne B. Blanding-Hurley

An advocate of literature that addresses the concerns and issues of women, Adrienne resides in Miami, Florida with her husband Harold and son James Allen. While contributing to this book, Adrienne found the reflection process to be exhilarating.

Ebony M. Brown

Ebony resides in Accokeek, Maryland with her husband Paul. She loves to travel and enjoys spending quality time with her husband, as well as family and friends. She firmly believes that in all things, give God thanks. Her favorite motto is "No matter what you go through, enjoy the journey. For it is during the journey when character is developed.... and your character can ascend you to unimaginable places." Ebony received her undergraduate and graduate degrees from South Carolina State University. She is a member of Delta Sigma Theta Sorority, Inc.

Tanika H. Campbell

Tanika is a former math teacher and actuarial analyst who enjoys reading, crocheting, and traveling in her spare time. She currently resides in Kailua, Hawaii with her husband Timothy and their newborn son, Timothy, Jr. Tanika holds undergraduate and graduate degrees from South Carolina State University and The Ohio State University, respectively. She utilized this book as an opportunity to recall the experiences that have shaped her life.

Azure Davis

Azure is a Graphic Designer from Atlanta, Georgia who currently resides in the Chicago area. She is also the artist behind the "Smashing Tomatoes" book cover design. Her alma mater is Spelman College. In addition to creative endeavors, Azure enjoys reading and traveling.

Tracy "Imani" Lynne Davis

The late Tracy "Imani" Lynne Davis was a charismatic and vivacious woman with a heart of gold. Prior to her tragic demise on April 27, 2005, Imani embraced the essence of womanhood with grace and possessed an inner beauty that was admirable. Adored by many, she was a loving mother, cousin, sister, grandmother, aunt, friend, and mentor. Imani was also blessed with an artistic talent to write poetry. In fact, the last poem that she wrote before her demise titled "Prosperity Principle" is featured as the book's Poetic Interlude. Imani was a native of Philadelphia, PA, but also enjoyed traveling abroad. Her spirit lives through every page of our book.

Wanda D. Davis

Wanda is an ambitious and motivated woman who wears many hats. Her passion for change has enabled her to serve on some of the most high profile political campaigns over the last decade, including working for U.S. Senatorial Candidate Harvey Gantt of Charlotte, NC in 1996, working for North Carolina Congressman Mel Watt in his historic victory in 1998, and working with Philadelphia, PA Mayor John F. Street in 2003. An extremely talented poet, Wanda wrote both the poetic prelude and poetic postlude featured in the book. In addition to serving as the book's Publicist, Wanda is the CEO of EweNique Productions, LLC and the Executive Director of the Julmani Foundation. This organization was founded in honor of her late mother Julia and late sister Tracy "Imani" Lynne Davis, author of the book's Poetic Interlude. Wanda is the proud mother of a six year-old model and actor, Elijah K. Davis. She resides in Philadelphia, PA and is a member of Delta Sigma Theta Sorority, Incorporated, along with a host of other civic and social organizations. She is a graduate of Bennett College. She received her B.S. degree from South Carolina State University and her M.S. degree from Virginia Tech.

Hope L. Doe

Hope currently resides in Charlotte, NC. She is an executive with a global management and technology consulting company. Hope enjoys traveling, entertaining, event planning, and spending time with family and friends. She hopes the book will provide insight and encouragement to women. She also hopes it will provide men with a unique look at various perspectives as seen through the eyes of women. Hope is a member of Alpha Kappa Alpha Sorority, Incorporated.

Sherice Langs Dowling

Sherice is an Accountant at a private corporation in Atlanta, GA. She, along with her husband Kyle are the proud parents of three sons: Deion, Kameron, and Brandon. Sherice firmly believes that experiences help to mold people into who they are. She viewed the experience of working with the co-authors as full-filling because it helped her with self-assessment as it relates to the world around her. Sherice's interests include health, fitness, and spending time with family and friends. She currently resides in Stone Mountain, Georgia.

Chrissie Ellis-Goodman

Currently residing in Columbia, South Carolina, Chrissie loves to read inspirational books and spending time with her husband and daughter. Her participation in this book project enabled her to contribute her perspective as a woman who has overcome adversity. She hopes that women will realize that despite the trials and tribulations they may encounter, success is possible. Chrissie's interests include real estate and web page design.

Natalie Jones

A resident of Atlanta, Georgia, Natalie's interests include reading inspirational articles, traveling, listening to jazz, and being a mother and wife to her husband Cleon and son Myles. Natalie is a Registered Nurse who manages a unit in one of Atlanta's premier hospitals. She is currently pursuing a Master's degree in Nursing. The words she lives by are "be not weary in well doing, for in due season you shall reap, if you faint not."

Yolanda Kennedy

A resident of Ellenwood, Georgia, Yolanda enjoys exercising, reading, traveling, and hanging out with friends and family. Her life philosophy is "always set your goals and dreams high, for you are the only one who can limit your abilities in reaching those goals."

NKenya Lassiter

NKenya resides in the Washington DC Metropolitan area. Her hobbies include reading and listening to reggae music. She is also an avid fan of baseball and football. She viewed this book project as a positive journey because it provided insight into how she approached various life experiences. She is a firm believer that "just because your approach to achieving a goal does not fit into a cookie cutter model, does not mean your goal is unreachable."

LaRonda J. Robinson

LaRonda is native of Beaufort, South Carolina. She currently resides in Columbia, SC. Her hobbies include reading, entertaining, and exploring. She loves to try new things and travel with her husband Warren. Her philosophy of life is "to love God totally ... to love self properly ... and to love others compassionately." What she enjoyed most about contributing to this book was the absolute freedom to express herself.

Dr. Sheriase Q. Sanders

A native of Atlanta, Georgia, Sheriase is currently a biology professor at a four-year university. Her hobbies include reading, sewing, skiing, exercising, mentoring, and traveling. She is a member of Delta Sigma Theta Sorority, Incorporated.

Dr. Marva Tutt

Marva is a native and resident of Augusta, Georgia. She is currently employed as the Principal of Augusta's "first" charter school. She is an active member of the Augusta community, and as a result was recently named a recipient of the Outstanding Vision Award sponsored by Aquarius Vision. Marva is the Co-Founder of a non-profit organization for inner-city young ladies called Girls Tyme and a member of Alpha Kappa Alpha Sorority, Incorporated. In her spare time, she enjoys reading, writing, traveling, and shopping. Marva's ultimate goal is to become a School Superintendent.

Poetic Prelude
"Smashing Your Tomatoes"

Have you ever had your tomatoes smashed?
And did you take it like a champ?
Have you ever smashed someone's tomatoes?
And got pasted like a stamp?

You see, this subject is very touchy,
Not something everyone can handle,
No need to get all Huffy
Girl, just kick off those sandals!

In most cases they keep it real,
It's not usually meant to hurt,
Smashing Tomatoes tells how one feels,
It may even reveal a little dirt!

If you've ever had your tomatoes smashed,
It may have been for your own good.
Sometimes it stings like whip lash,
Why not appreciate it…. If you would!

Girl don't you take it personally,
I'm just putting it on the Money

Because I love you unconditionally,
DON'T MEAN TO "SMASH YOUR TOMATOES, HONEY"!

PART I

LIFE'S PERSPECTIVES FROM A–K

AMBITION

"It's easier to keep striving when you have someone else beside you striving too. It's so encouraging to know that you are not alone in your journey."

"When it knocks at your door, you must be prepared to let it in and go wherever it takes you!"

Ahhhh? ambition! We sing your praises and seek to possess you! People often speak of ambition as a magnificent attribute all of us should strive for, but is it? Supposedly the possession of this trait promises victory and success, but does it? In order for ambition to live up to its lofty reputation, it must originate from the right place. If not, ambition is nothing more than an empty promise. Think about your goals. What is behind your drive to aspire for these things? Is it society, family, your husband or lover? What about greed, envy, resentment, or rivalry?

Are you seeking to gratify yourself or someone else? There will always be someone willing to offer an opinion on what you should do, what you should be, or what you should want! These opinions may even provide valuable advice and constructive criticism. But the truth of the matter is you are the only person who knows what you want out of life. Therefore, you are the only person who can evaluate your own desires and motivations. In the end you're the one who must live with the outcome of your choices. Know what lies behind your ambitions and question the goals you have chosen. Where were you in your life when you created your goals? Most importantly, will you actually be happy if and when you achieve the goals you have set? If you don't like your answers, then perhaps your ambition is futile. I have asked myself these questions, and there have been times when I was dissatisfied with my answers. Sometimes I think I would be closer to achieving the goals I desire if I stopped allowing others to convince me to do otherwise. There are also times when I lacked ambition because I didn't truly believe in my goal. I welcome the advice of others, but want my aspirations to originate from within. Contentment in the pursuit of my goals even in the face of temporary failures and setbacks comes from knowing what I want and why. I want to know that my ambition is leading me to the place I want to be. Where is your ambition leading you?

Ambition has been the very crux of my success as a woman. There have been numerous times in my life when I dreamed of opportunities that soon became mine as the result of my ambitious nature. Ambition is the inner car that drives me to accomplish the goals that I desire whether personal or professional. A woman who possesses ambition ultimately possesses the ability to accomplish any goal that she undertakes despite the obstacles she might encounter. Ambition is about making things happen, not discussing how they could happen or should have happened. It emerges from an intrinsic motivation that many only hear about, but never experience. It is the quality that separates the mediocre from the superb. While many adore ambition, few possess it. By confronting our inner feelings, we can tune into our inner desires and in turn can pursue them. To some ambition is only used when they wish to obtain something. However, in order to make the best out of our life experiences, we must utilize each minute, hour, and moment of the day to pursue happiness. As no day is promised to us, God has given us the gift of ambition to use while on earth. It is through ambition that we can begin to enjoy life and our choice to use it now or later. Unfortunately, our decision to use it later could mean never having the opportunity to use it. Each day we awaken, we must take advantage of the opportunities that await us. Ambition means seizing the opportunity, seizing the moment, and seizing success. When it knocks at your door, you must be prepared to let it in and go wherever it takes you! It is often said that ambitious women rule the world. Don't stifle your ambition, embrace it and allow it to flourish. A life without ambition is a life without complete fulfillment. Leave no stone unturned and live vicariously through yourself. Whether it's a new job or an opportunity to try a new experience, don't allow your fears to hinder your ambitions. You are capable of accomplishing any goal you desire. Remember, you are a woman of distinction and a creature of power. The world awaits your ambitions.

I have always been ambitious. Even as a child I always wanted to do more and achieve more. I have to give a majority of the thanks to my parents because they did an awesome job of setting the parameters of "*I can*" and "*I will*," and never those of failure, doubt or fear. My three main ambitions in life are to become financially affluent, have total personal freedom, and in turn help as many people as I can to gain these gifts. I don't believe you can catch ambition, I believe it is inherent. A person may not always act as if they possess ambition, but given the right influence and nourishment that seed of ambition can grow. I believe a large portion of what we hear during any given day originates from our own lips. It therefore makes sense to me that my words are those that need to be the most guarding. This way I assure that I will not intentionally or unintentionally defeat myself through negative language.

I have always envisioned myself doing something meaningful and extraordinary with my life, even when I had no idea of what direction I was going. I have always enjoyed reading books about people that I admired and could relate to on a personal level—people who have made a difference in the world. In time, I had the opportunity to meet astounding people who would become my peers. They have fueled the development of my ambition. Likewise, the influence of my mentors has molded me into the person I am today. My mentors helped me gain confidence in myself. My mother always emphasized how important it was for me to have goals beyond graduating from high school. I am proud to be a second-generation college graduate, and I owe a lot of my accomplishments to my mother. She influenced me not just through her words, but also by her actions. She was independent, smart, confident, strong and fearless. I started to recognize my strengths and weaknesses by being around the right people. It's easier to keep striving when you have someone else beside you striving too. It's so encouraging to know that you are not alone in your journey.

Ambition is usually a positive attribute. However, it can sometimes be destructive to a household unit. In many cases ambitious people make selfish partners. Despite their intentions to provide for their families, they sometimes become more enthralled with accomplishing their own goals and place the needs of their families on the back of the stove. Like anything else, the dosage of ambition should be moderate. Strive to be ambitious, but not to the detriment of your family and the people you love most.

I often find interacting with very ambitious people to be intimidating. Overall, I think I'm a fairly motivated person, but I think calling myself ambitious would definitely be a stretch of reality. A lot of the ambitious people that I interact with don't seem to enjoy life. They often concentrate so much on becoming successful that they rarely have the time or energy to appreciate the rewards that their ambition has granted them. I'm perplexed … why in the world would people want to spend most of their lives working hard to get to the top only to discover that they won't have anyone at the top to share their success with? I have seen numerous ambitious people abandon their families, friends, and personal interests, just so they can boast about their ambitions and achievements. I'm not concerned at all about being ambitious if doing so means that I will have to live my life always placing my interests on the back burner. Life is too short and I want to live it while I can!

BEAUTY

"I want to feel completely comfortable with myself, and not bound to other's standards of beauty."

"Self-confident and secure women who are comfortable within always project a certain element of beauty."

Unfortunately, in this society beauty plays a big role. With the rise of plastic surgery and people trying to look like celebrities, I think the standard of beauty has been raised to unrealistic expectations. The focus on cosmetic surgery is sending a subtle message to women that if they don't like the way they look, they can simply "fix" themselves through surgery. Recently, I read an article that stated teenagers today equate having plastic surgery to having their teeth cleaned!

Although I have never seriously considered plastic surgery, I have found myself considering ways that I can achieve the enviable physique or attributes of someone who has undergone these procedures. Eventually, I had to look at myself and discover what was best for me. This meant slowly getting into a regular exercise regimen, eating healthier, and not allowing the use of a chemical process on my hair. Honestly, these changes took some time to get used to, and I had to undergo many inner battles of self-doubt and self-consciousness. But through it all, I feel I look better than ever and am learning to accept the "real" me. I want the sense of accomplishment that comes from working hard to exercise the weight off and maintain it. I want to feel completely comfortable with myself, and not bound to other's standards of beauty. There are also times when I have considered liposuction. These are thoughts I battled with daily throughout my personal journey to feeling more beautiful.

In my struggle to define beauty, I have discovered that one has to learn to accept and ultimately love herself. Self-confident and secure women who are comfortable within always project a certain element of beauty. In addition, I have learned that relying on others to validate your beauty will always be self-defeating. Plenty of people have gone to drastic extremes in the quest for beauty and the attention it brings, only to discover they cannot escape themselves. Through my experiences, it is clear to me that when you love yourself, you will treat others with the respect and love you expect for yourself. In turn, others will recognize this quality as beauty.

Our society places such a strong emphasis on beauty, and every woman has her own ideas about what beauty is. Some feel that breast lifts and tummy tucks will create beauty. Others think revealing an excessive amount of skin or being exceptionally thin is beauty. But a woman must first ask herself if beauty is from within or without. Everyone possesses some form of beauty. If you believe you are beautiful—then you are! You must take what God has given you and manifest it! I can honestly say that I consider myself to be beautiful inside and out. For one, I was raised to have a healthy self-image and I believe that is 100% of the battle. The battle is either won or lost in your mind, the rest is just a formality. Once you believe in something and have conviction, nobody can take that away from you. If I felt I needed it—and that it would help me feel better about myself and my self-image—I would spare no length to make myself more attractive. Appearance has definitely helped me along in life. In all honesty, I believe men and women who are perceived to have a pleasing appearance get more breaks than those who are not perceived in that way. I believe my physical attractiveness has opened many doors for me. However, once I enter those doors, I let loose who I really am. My personal opinion is that the cliché "beauty is skin deep" is just a little outdated. Maybe this phrase was a little more appropriate prior to the manufacturing of make up. I honestly do not think our society functions off of the same philosophy. I don't think this mindset is realistic. While I personally know plenty of people who verbally profess to live by this ideal, I know very few who actually do. I surely do not believe anyone actually pursues a relationship with someone who is unattractive, at least not without an ulterior motive. Who would actually desire for their offspring, the inheritance of unattractiveness? I don't see any hands raised and I surely don't hear any voices. The answer to me is quite clear—our society loves individuals who are physically attractive. Most interesting is that everyone can gain the benefits of what I deem the "cutie theory." Everyone is attractive to someone, which to me equates to everyone reaping the benefits that beauty has to offer.

Contrarily, don't expect every beautiful person you see to model this type of behavior. It seems as though many times the spirit of outer beauty is accompanied by an inner unattractiveness, which I have found in many cases to be insecurity. It may seem ridiculous that someone who possesses so many extrinsically aesthetic qualities could be insecure, but it is fairly common.

Look all around you; people who are perceived as attractive are usually treated better than their counterparts. Even without consciously making a decision to revere them in a higher regard, we give them that extra point because we think they're attractive. I have no problem admitting that I possess strong superficial qualities. What's more important to me is that I learn to deal with this issue in a reasonable manner. If it seems as if I'm being unreasonably judgmental of the "fine and divine" or that I have smashed your tomatoes too brutally, please forgive me. As a human being I have weaknesses, some of which I can alter and others that I simply don't want to, and will not consider changing. Then again, maybe my attraction to the attractive is not the result of my inadequacy, but instead the result of a society whose values I have engulfed. While you ponder on that thought, I'm off to the gym—where eye candy is plentiful.

I am beautiful, I am beautiful … yes I am. But if this is true, then why don't I feel this way. Why do I work so hard to become beautiful and desirable by all, only to find out that I'm not? When I was young, I allowed my beauty to be defined by the way others viewed me. Even when I thought I was pretty, there was always someone who felt I wasn't. Believe it or not, but I have actually contemplated undergoing cosmetic surgery to fix some of the imperfections that others seem to notice on a daily basis. But even if I fix these imperfections, I realize that I will not be repairing the real issue—my psychological imperfections. I must first alter the way I perceive my beauty, before I can feel beautiful. So today

I'm removing all of the beauty supplements that society has convinced me I should have in order to be beautiful—hair extensions, colored contact lenses, and artificial nails. I don't need any of these falsities to make me feel beautiful and neither do you. Remember, when God created you, he didn't make any mistakes. He made you beautiful at birth and certainly doesn't need your assistance now with altering his masterpiece. When you make adjustments to the way God made you, you are hindering your beauty. Furthermore, you are showing him that you doubt his ability to make you into the creature you are supposed to be. Stop and take a look at how beautiful you are, and by all means stop allowing others to define your beauty standards. You are already beautiful. You just need to realize it!

Am I beautiful? Well, at least some days I am. Let's be real … some days I think I am beautiful and some days I don't. Sometimes, I wear make-up, hair extensions, wigs, and a girdle. Why? Because I want to look better. You may be able to relate to those days when you just know you look good. Your hair looks wonderful, your make-up is flawless, and your outfit fits perfectly. When you look good, you feel good; you feel beautiful. I know I couldn't possibly be the only one who scurries past the mirror when I'm naked. I'm not happy with my body all of the time and sometimes I just don't feel beautiful. Is it wrong that I like to use external accessories or that I sometimes consider cosmetic surgery? We all want to believe that we are beautiful, but even with the strongest self-esteem, we can't ignore what's in the mirror. Can I say that I really love my "jelly belly" or my chubby cheeks? Of course, there are things we wish were different about our bodies, but this doesn't mean we don't ultimately love ourselves or think that we are beautiful. Intrinsically, there needs to be a balance between beauty and a healthy self-image. I hate seeing people prescribe to the latest "look" at the expense of their health. Beauty is a journey that takes some of us longer to get there than others. Along the way, we will encounter detours, hills, and valleys, but when we get comfortable in our own skin, we realize we're finally there.

I think beauty is being 'OK' with me, even if from time to time I might need a little help from my girdle.

CAMARADERIE

"My friends inspire me ... we inspire each other to do great things!"

"The role my friends play in my life can be equated to my jewelry—each one has a special way of accessorizing my soul."

Friendship is very important to me. I believe everyone needs companionship, support, and guidance from those outside of the family. A different kind of bond is developed during friendships and it improves your quality of life. Throughout my life, I've been able to develop friendships surrounding similar goals and interests. My old and new friendships have provided me with new insight and guidance through my life journeys. The insight and guidance that I receive from my friends allows me to be a productive person in society. My friendships are a big part of who I am, as well as how successful I have become. Without support from my friends, it would have been difficult to go through the struggles and problems I have encountered. I am constantly reminded of the blessings my friendships have granted me. Who knows where I would be today without my friends.

Friendships are an integral part of my being. It is funny that my mother always told me that I didn't need anyone except myself. She said I shouldn't depend on anyone to make me happy. But when you're sad, who is going to be the person to help you feel better? Everyone needs somebody in this world and I think that is what friends are for. If I didn't have friends, I'm not sure where I would be today. My friendships have changed a great deal throughout my life. This can be attributed to how I have evolved as a woman. When I was younger, I called everyone my friend. I hung in groups of no less than 8 girls. I assumed girls I saw alone didn't have friends, and those that had only one or two probably weren't well liked either. Basically, it was all about popularity. As I've matured, I've lost and gained friends. In fact, most of my old friendships no longer exist. However, I don't regret those old friendships because I've learned from each one. Life would be quite different without the friends that I have. I probably wouldn't be a very good friend myself. Friends can sometimes teach you how to truly be a friend, not in words but through their actions. My friends come from different backgrounds and have different career paths. My friends inspire me ... we inspire each other to do great things!

Imagine waking up one day only to discover that all of your friends had been killed in a tragic accident. Sounds pretty brutal, huh? Have you ever stopped to evaluate which friends you'd miss, if any, and why? When I think of my friendships, I think of the unique and individual bonds that I have with each friend. Believe it or not, but I have actually had friendships that never invoked in me a feeling of connection. Needless to say, over the years, I have realized that a friend is someone whose companionship you should enjoy and long for. When I reflect upon these mere acquaintances, I become disgusted with no one, but myself. However, my displeasure is not out of vengeance, it is my way of actualizing the energy and time I wasted on "so-called friends"; people whom today are absolutely of no value to my life. However, not all of my experiences with these acquaintances can be written off as inadequate. Through these malfunctions, I believe I was blessed with the opportunity to differentiate between friendships and acquaintanceships.

In retrospect, I must admit that less than 20% of the individuals I called my friends, had actually worked to earn the title. I have since become more stringent in the friendship selection process; only few can even qualify for tryouts. After years of enduring dysfunctional friendships, I feel I have finally reached the pinnacle of my friendship circle. At the present time, I can honestly say that I am no longer accepting applications—I feel I have enough friends. I have been blessed to accumulate in my inner circle a myriad of self-sufficient and positive women who possess the ability to change the world. When you think of friendship, it is important to consider the notion in an unconditional manner. Alike any healthy relationship, when you can visualize yourself still wanting to maintain a friendship even after a dispute, you know your friendship will last the long haul. A true friendship means making sacrifices to make your friend happy or avoiding certain actions that make a friend unhappy. We should be very selective with whom we chose to call our friends. We can't just issue this title to anyone. We instead must examine the connection we have, if any, with the individual before we can stamp him or her with the seal of friendship approval. The next time you're close to calling someone your friend, be certain to confirm whether this person is in your first, second, or third inner circle. Don't be afraid to be picky. After all, contrary to your family members, friends are actually people whom you can select. So before you deem someone as your friend, make sure you measure the circumference of your circle. If your circle consists of individuals who don't add value to your portfolio, then you need to begin accepting new applicants. In our lifetime, we must surround ourselves with positive individuals whose values are similar to our own, but not necessarily a replica. If someone's relationship is not meaningful to you, then you must release him or her from your circle. Most importantly, when selecting friends you should avoid people whose connection is only based upon your convenience to them. Most essential to an effective friendship is filling your circle with those who will be honest and upfront with you; shamelessly challenging your views whenever necessary. The role my friends play in my life can be equated to my jewelry—each one has a special way of accessorizing my soul.

Who you will become is greatly influenced by who you befriend. Eliminating toxic friendships is one of the best decisions you can make in your mission to become a better person. I often review my list of friends and reflect upon how blessed I am to be surrounded by such powerful women of virtue who inspire me to reach my potential. True friends can add value and purpose to your life. Anyone who subtracts positive value from your life is definitely not your friend. You deserve to be surrounded by positive people who are supportive of your goals and want for you nothing, but the absolute best. If you find that your "so called" friends are adding destruction to your life, then you need to consider subtracting them from your life. In your quest to become the person you are destined to become make sure you are calling the right people your friends. People who limit their own destiny will only try to limit yours. A true friend never wants you to settle for a life that is mediocre.

He or she will motivate you to not only reach for the stars, but touch them!

Over the years, I have been faced with numerous challenges regarding my friendships. Of these lessons, the most important has been my discovery that not all friendships are everlasting; some are seasonal. Although I am regretful that the seasons for many of my friendships have passed, I am grateful for the blessings that these friendships have bestowed upon my life. Whether the friendships exposed me to new experiences or led me to other friendships, I have become a better person as a result of them. Good friends will stand the test of time and those who don't pass this test will eventually fade in time. The value of camaraderie is to be appreciated and never taken for granted; it is a two-way street. So, the next time you ponder upon the thoughts of camaraderie, remember not to ask yourself what your friends can do to be better friends to you, but instead what you can do to be a better friend to them.

DATING

"To date or not to date, that is the question."

"The down side of dating is going on date after date after date ... and kissing lots of frogs before you meet your prince. It can be exhausting!"

To date or not to date, that is the question. Most women have faced this dilemma at some point in their dating lives. Dating is an emotional rollercoaster carrying us from excitement and anxiousness to disappointment and frustration. It was usually in those moments of frustration that I swore off dating forever. Thankfully, that was a promise I didn't keep. It was on those rollercoaster rides that I learned the most about myself. I learned that I had self-esteem issues, looked for validation from other people, and really didn't know what I wanted in a mate. Did I want someone who was fine, funny, spiritual, successful, aggressive, shy, nice, or adventurous?

Like many women, I thought I knew what I was looking for in a mate. As I grew older, I realized that I needed a person who was just as versatile as I was; someone who would accept me unconditionally. It was my worst dating experience that prepared me to accept and appreciate the love I am receiving today. At my lowest point, I thought I would never get married or find someone to connect with on a spiritual, emotional, and physical level. The happiness I feel today was worth any pain I ever felt before. It was only when I was ready for love that "Mr. Right" came into my life. Today, I am engaged to a man who is not only my friend, but treats me like a queen and loves me unconditionally. At no other point in time would I have been ready for the love my fiancé had to offer. I couldn't make it happen when I thought I was ready, but it happened when GOD knew I was ready. As with any rollercoaster ride, a downfall is always followed by an up. So, I would say to any woman currently dating … enjoy the ride as much as you can. Of course, this is always easier said than done.

It is important to identify what you are looking for in terms of dating a person, and to determine what you would like the end result to be. This can prevent confusion and emotional turmoil later if the relationship should progress. Women have the tendency to allow their emotions to surface too soon or to create unrealistic fantasies when they believe they have met that perfect person. At times, we become overwhelmed with the belief that we have met the proverbial prince charming, and ignore red flags that could prevent wasting time and energy on something that will not last. One of the biggest mistakes I have seen women make in the dating game is becoming intimate too soon. Taking your time to get to know the other person is vitally important when it comes to allowing someone into your personal space. Sharing too much information too soon on previous relationship mishaps can also be lethal when trying to develop a new relationship. In my opinion, women could benefit from spending more time listening and less time talking. Performing a quick interview during the first five minutes of meeting someone can tell you a lot. As I reflect on dating, I can truly say that I must have been successful because after dating the same person exclusively for about six years, the end result for me was marriage.

How do I feel about dating … hmmm, as I ponder the thought the first word that comes to mind is DIFFICULT. I should start off by saying that I don't think dating itself is hard, but that it is difficult to date someone who sparks my interest. Dating was much easier when I was in my earlier twenties because I now have higher standards. I have become more serious about dating, and my motivation has changed. I want to find a long-term relationship and eventually get married. I am not dating anyone at this time, and I do feel like this is somewhat my own fault. I have put other priorities ahead of dating and meeting new people. Just thinking of the dating process scares me. Of course, dating has its pros and cons. Going out can be fun because you have the opportunity to make new friends and possibly meet a potential mate. Dating also provides the opportunity to discover what qualities you like in men and those qualities you don't. The down side of dating is going on date after date after date and kissing lots of frogs before you meet your prince. It can be an exhausting process!

It is amazing that online dating has become so popular. Is it getting that hard to meet people? I haven't quite gotten the courage to meet someone through online dating, but I have heard good stories and bad stories. One day I might feel a little more comfortable with the concept. Until then I want to meet men the old-fashioned way.

Although I have been married for several years now, I often reminisce with my single girlfriends about my dating years. Contrary to the experiences had by many of my friends, I absolutely enjoyed dating. In fact, I believe my dating experiences allowed me to better appreciate meeting my husband. It is my belief that women who don't invest enough time into dating are placing themselves at an unfair disadvantage. Dating provides women with the opportunity to grow, self-reflect, and learn. I don't regret any of the dating experiences that I've had. In fact, I value these experiences. For it was these experiences that taught me invaluable lessons about myself, my desires, and my needs.

I view dating as an opportunity to taste test God's creations. It is also an unpredictable, but yet invigorating experience that you should be prepared for before you take the plunge. Many women grunt at the thought of dating because not only is it time consuming, but competitive. Of course it is … with so many "dateables" to choose from one must prepare to compete or be timed-out. Comparable to the game of chess, you must learn to make the right move or risk being put out of the game or even worse captured. Then again, maybe being captured is your next move. In this case, you must proceed with caution, but by all means let your move be known to your opponent. The bottom line is communicating your thoughts and making sure those thoughts are consistent with your actions. However, please be informed that sometimes too quick a notification, may lead you down the path to Loneliness Avenue. It may be worth the time to wait things out until you are 100% certain of your intentions. Many women date aimlessly, not knowing the goal of their pursuit. Alike any other task, in order to be successful you must first identify your mission. If you are interested in dating with the intention of marriage, then don't neglect voicing your opinion. However, I must advise you to refrain from making this proclamation on the first date. Surely, you'll want to give the relationship time to marinade just to ensure that this discussion is necessary for your next move. The risk of prematurely discussing your dating intentions with a candidate you are unsure of is quite simple—your honesty about wanting a long term relationship may be sending mixed signals regarding your interest in moving forward with that individual. As desperate times call for desperate measures, I have seen many women long to go out on a date so badly that they lower their standards. Soon their cry to simply meet someone becomes their cry to escape from an unwanted relationship.

I can personally attest to the consequences of being too upfront too quickly. With a low level of dating disaster tolerance, at the conclusion of a rather quiet evening, I quickly issued my date a pink slip. To my surprise, he quickly issued one to me in return. My thoughts of course were "wow, that wasn't supposed to happen." Needless to say, most effective for me was a dose of my own medicine before I began regretting my hasty decision-making. Such a nice guy, but things just didn't seem to be working out. Hmm, was it something wrong with me or with him? Was I too finicky a dater? Well, as the story goes, months later we were engaged and are now married. So, when you begin feeling sorry for yourself because you haven't had a date in weeks, think about all of the "delightful dateables" you pass during the course of a day. Then consider all of the "dateables" you have access to and others you have passed up because you have served them on a silver platter to an opponent. In actuality, it may be your own fault for the dating episodes in which you star. Everyone is dateable to someone. It is up to you to figure out who's dateable to you. The key to this quest is deciding for yourself the qualities that you seek in a mate. Contrary to what your family members and friends may tell you, only you truly know who is right for you. As you explore your options, remember your delightful and dateable prospect may be waiting around the corner for you.

For a number of reasons, I have gone for over three years without seriously dating. I am a thirty-something year-old woman who values life and relationships and would like to meet someone to share my love with. However, achieving that goal can be a difficult one, especially when dating is the avenue most must travel to reach that destination. Over the years, my dating expectations have changed as I have experienced many dating pleasantries and nightmares. Initially, as an adult I dated with the goal of getting married in mind. In the process, I was sometimes blinded by good looks, charming ways, or because I masked my true feelings. However, due to some candid coaching I received from girlfriends "who smashed my tomatoes" and challenged me to alter my dating strategies, I began to alter my outlook. The advice of these women proved useful: 1) smile, 2) slow down, 3) remove dating limitations, 4) don't be afraid to make the first move, and 5) establish intentions early on. A little wiser and more confident in who I am and what I want, I now know what I can and cannot handle. I am not afraid to start over, move outside of my comfort zone and live a little on the edge. I can truly say that since I have used my experiences, lessons, coaching, and approached dating with an open mind.... things are starting to look up.

What fond memories come to mind when I think about my dating years. I recall taking the time to pick out the right outfit or buying a new tube of lipstick. Dating allows you to learn about the person you are building a relationship with and about yourself. Good relationships allow us to better ourselves and push us closer to success. On the contrary, bad relationships can tear us down and prevent us from fully appreciating our wonderfulness. Nothing bothers me more than when I see someone staying in a relationship where both parties argue all the time, degrade each other, and make each other feel worthless. You don't need any extra help in being made to feel less than the best. Dating should be viewed as a great learning experience.

ETHICS

"It has been my experience that you don't truly understand the weight of your values until they are tested. Values are strong when they are consistent with everything you have experienced or will experience."

"Maintaining a strong value system becomes increasingly important as we face complex issues like religion, sexual morality and autonomy. Be true to your values and know their origin"

Everyday I am faced with challenges, in which my personal and professional ethics are tested. It seems as though our society is constantly setting up roadblocks of temptation. However, I urge you to resist these temptations no matter how enticing they may be. No one can ever be certain when and where eyes are watching. A mere glimpse at the daily news even reveals our society's lack of integrity. It even seems that individuals who hold positions of authority have succumb to the pressures of these values.

I cannot emphasize enough the importance of sticking to your own values and not saturating them with the ethics that seem right to others. It will be you who will have to live with the decisions you make and their consequences. In our weakest moments we yearn for approval and affirmation, but we must always remember that the most important lesson of all is maintaining our personal integrity. It is a responsibility that we must always take seriously.

It's amazing how people will try to manipulate you in order to get what they want, but only if you allow them to do so. The bigger picture is that you must be courageous enough to stand firm on your own values, even when you have to stand in solitude. You should never risk sacrificing your integrity for anyone. Whether you face losing a job, a relationship, or money, more valuable to you then succumbing to the pressures of unethical behavior, is your reputation and dignity. After all, with your dignity and integrity you will be able to regain your material assets. Without these attributes, you may never be given another chance for redemption.

Most of my values are Christian based. I was raised in a home that instilled these values in me, and I try to incorporate these values into my life daily. I think about the impact of my decisions and try to treat people how they wish to be treated. It is hard at times to live up to all the values and standards of others, including family and friends. Judgment can be clouded and making decisions based on selfish needs versus for the benefit of others is always a possibility. We are all human and mistakes and misjudgments are made. What really matters is that we recognize those mistakes and misjudgments and work to correct them. It is definitely a constant battle.

As with many other women, most of my values have originated from my family. As children though, we do not think of them as values, but rather as rules or expectations. You just know that you are expected to treat people a certain way and respect adults. As a child, my family was responsible for defining what was good or evil, true or false. It has been my experience that you don't truly understand the weight of your values until they are tested. Values are strong when they are consistent with everything you have experienced or will experience. They are reference points that help us in situations that place us at risk.

My values were solidified in college. I encountered new ideas, and people from different cultures and socio-economic backgrounds. College allowed me to shape my own ideas, recognize my position on certain issues, and act in accordance with my beliefs. I can recall being in positions where my values were compromised. I participated in activities that went against my value system and later made me appear weak primarily because I decided to follow the group instead of my own principles. I later decided that I was a role model not a follower, and decided to make wiser choices.

I also learned the hard lesson that my values weren't necessarily shared or considered to be the best by others. I had always thought that my values were the TRUTH. I believed that if you were doing something that went against my values then you were wrong. I remember my first encounter with an atheist … ooh my goodness. It was in college and my first instinct was to disassociate myself from this person. And you know, I told her that she was going straight to hell for denying God. Why?

Because "I" valued God and He was #1 according to my system. When I discussed this with my father, he reminded me that although I disagreed with the beliefs of this person, I should remember the fact that my values did not have to become her values.

Our values will be refined as we age and encounter new friends. Maintaining a strong value system becomes increasingly important as we face complex issues like religion, sexual morality and autonomy. Be true to your values and know their origin. Values repeatedly affect our lives and will sustain us when times are hard.

When dating, do you feel like you have to hide who you really are to gain a relationship? Do you change your personality to be liked? Do you acquire new hobbies and interests to win affection? Being ethical is being truthful, being honest, and doing what is right. When dating, it is important not only to be honest with your partner, but with yourself as well. You must be honest enough to admit what you like and don't like in your partner. You must be honest about your value system, your aspirations, and your ideals. Being ethical means being truthful about what your expectations and goals are in a relationship. In essence, ethics in a relationship means trusting yourself enough to know when a relationship is right for you or that you need to "give it up, turn it loose," and "let it go" if it doesn't work for YOU!

On a good day, I walk a straight line; never wavering on my ethical beliefs. However, on the other days, I struggle to prevent from my ethics from blowing away in the wind. It seems like my goals would be easier to achieve if I just played some of the "dirty" games many of my colleagues play—lying, cheating, backbiting, and backstabbing. When I look to my left and right, I see that wrongdoing in my workplace environment is prevalent. Then when I look up, I remember who is looking over my shoulder. At that very moment, I am reminded that the fast route to success always leads to a roadblock. Although it often seems that people who possess good ethics are the last to finish the race, it is our ethics that help us to jump over hurdles of dishonesty and dodge javelins of deceit that are thrown our way. People with good ethics always reach the finish line first in the race we call life.

FAITH

"You demonstrate an act of faith each time you board a plane. You believe that it will take you to your destination, but you have no proof of it. You have entrusted your life to unknown pilots and mechanics. That's faith. Believe and receive."

"Faith is the substance of things hoped for, the evidence of things not seen."

Hold on! Be strong! Don't give up! When I think of faith, I think of it in a spiritual sense. To have faith is to believe, trust or to rely on something or someone. Faith, for me, is knowing without seeing and believing without fully understanding. If you are a Christian, as I am, you may connect your faith to God alone. But faith extends to our families, children and society as a whole. We must be faithful to our loved ones, we must work to keep our promises and remain authentic or truthful. It is always wonderful to hear from a friend that says, "I knew I could count on you" or "you never let me down." This challenges me to remain faithful to those around me.

It is difficult to explain my faith to others, but it is easier to show them. People can see whether or not you are faithful. I challenge those of you who believe you have little faith to reflect upon this thought: You demonstrate an act of faith each time you board a plane. You believe that it will take you to your destination, but you have no proof of it. You have entrusted your life to unknown pilots and mechanics. That's faith. Believe and receive.

"Faith is the substance of things hoped for, the evidence of things not seen." Faith can be interpreted in many ways. Some interpret it religiously or in association with another person. Having faith religiously requires understanding the principles of your religion and having the will to incorporate those ideas and principles into your life.

Having faith in humans is a little different. Faith in this sense requires trust in another individual. This person could be a parent, child, husband, wife, girlfriend, boyfriend, or best friend. Sometimes faith in humans may require allowing yourself to be vulnerable and possibly being hurt if they break the trust you've given. I have spoken to several women who state they will never believe in "a man" again. This is terrible that one man could change a women's perspective, faith, and trust in all men. How do we get our faith back in a man or a woman? That question seems to puzzle women as a whole, and I have not yet learned the answer. Faith in humans is complicated. Faith should be valued more. We all should do our part to restore and preserve the faith that someone may have in us.

My personal definition of faith is pretty simple; faith is acting on what you believe. There have been times when my faith faltered. It wasn't due to a lack of knowing what was right, but due to a lack of confidence. My goal is to never allow my faith to falter. I keep my faith by staying in the action state of life, and never watching from the sidelines. Whatever one's fear is, I believe taking action will cure it and turn it into faith.

My faith has definitely changed the way I view myself. Faith is such an important aspect of my family life and personal relationships. It not only allows us to have a deeper understanding of ourselves and others, but shapes who we are. I personally believe that when it comes to relationships, those that are unequally yoked will have a harder time keeping their relationship together. Our faith helps to define us; giving us parameters and a blueprint to work within in the game we call life.

Every person has a unique definition of faith. However, for each of us "having faith" involves believing in *something*. This something could be a person (such as yourself or a friend), a higher being, or an intangible concept like believing that everything happens for a reason. It is so easy to possess faith when things are going as we think they should. For most people, the greatest obstacle in faith is deciding what to do when our faith is challenged. When we are hurt, when things are not going our way, or when an event happens that doesn't neatly fit into our beliefs do we stop believing … or do we continue to have faith?

I personally faced such a challenge when the faith I have in the good of others was tested. After encountering several situations where people I liked and respected were being self-serving, deceitful, or hypocritical, I began to wonder if what I believed was foolish. I felt hurt and disappointed. In turn, I decided that believing in the good of others was a general waste of my time. I resolved to focus on only what I wanted and how I felt—whoever was not okay with this was simply baggage that could be replaced or discarded from my life. Changing my beliefs also changed my *attitude*. I took on a negative mindset and was not happy with the way my new attitude made me feel, nor did I enjoy the way in which I interacted with others as a result. I came to understand that my faith serves a valuable purpose: it shapes my attitude, perception of the world around me, and how I interact in that world. My belief in the good of others is not about controlling events in my life or predicting what people will do. It is about believing that, despite those bumps in the road, you will be able to see the good and will reflect that back out to others.

As a Christian woman, I believe in biblical principles. I have a belief and trust in God and I am confident in things that I can't always physically touch or see. Faith can be a difficult concept to grasp, but when you develop a relationship with God, the force of faith can be something so strong that you see the untouchable as touchable. Faith is a very important part of my life and has impacted me personally and professionally. There are times when you may not be sure of the right decision, but pray about it and make the decision that you think is best. Your faith tells you that although you don't know what will happen as a result of that decision, you believe that God knows what's best.

I took a step of faith when I quit my job to pursue another career opportunity. I left a world of financial security to begin a new career that had the potential to be very profitable. I am happy with the decision I made and believe my family is too. At the time, I wasn't sure that I was making the right decision, but had faith that things would work out. You can't just have faith for the sake of having faith, you have to put that faith to the test—exercise it. Sure, there will be times when we question the things that happen in our lives and we may start to lose faith; we're human so it's only natural. During these times, we may wonder if we have enough faith. The key is to keep the faith. Sometimes, we go through things, pleasant and unpleasant, to get to the place where we need to be. You have to believe that God only wants what's best for you!

In 2005, my faith was put to the test when my mother became very ill. Due to the extent of her illness, she required around-the-clock care. Within a ten-month time frame, my mother was in and out of the hospital eight times with various complications. Throughout the duration of my mother's illness, I struggled with understanding why God would allow this to happen to one of His best. I am a believer, but admit that my faith wavered during this journey. I prayed and believed that healing was going to occur, but did not see the manifestation. It took some time but I had to be reminded that God is omniscient and that He had a plan for my mother and our family. I now realize that God allowed this situation to happen because He had confidence that we could handle it. I believe the faith of my entire family and those who supported us during this challenging time has grown. Even though my faith weakened at times, my mother's didn't. In fact, it was her faith that encouraged me to persevere. Although my mother has not fully recovered physically, she remains encouraged and more determined than ever. I believe the purpose of this test was for me to testify of God's goodness, His faithfulness, and His power. I trust that there was a reason for my mother's illness, the lengthy healing process, and mounting financial struggles. I have faith that in time God will reveal his plan.

GLASS CEILINGS

"I believe sometimes you don't know that the ceiling exists because you can see through it. You see opportunity and don't know that there is a barrier until you hit your head."

"The very admittance of glass ceilings is a hindrance to success."

The Glass Ceiling is an idiom used to describe the conditions that prevent people—in most cases women—from achieving higher positions in corporate America. Some leaders in corporate America still believe that males should dominate in business and a woman's place is in the home. Women have to understand the politics that keep the glass ceiling in place. In order to advance, we must know how the corporate world operates. We must challenge ourselves, step out of the box, and move up that corporate ladder. In order to eradicate the glass ceiling, one must be willing to travel with a hammer at all times. I believe sometimes you don't know that the ceiling exists because you can see through it. You can see opportunity and don't know that there is a barrier until you hit your head. The pain will either discourage or motivate you to take out your hammer and shatter the ceiling. As women, it is important that we realize our goals are achievable. We must commit to following these goals through to fruition. After reading these statements, broken glass should be everywhere!

I first encountered the infamous glass ceiling while working as a student assistant in graduate school. While working alongside a male colleague, I was informed that he was being paid more than I, despite the fact that he wasn't required to work as many hours. I was furious and, surprisingly to me, he was very empathetic. My co-worker encouraged me to stand up for myself, and to seek equal treatment from the school's administration. Shortly thereafter, I talked with the appropriate person and the problem was immediately resolved. I was given equal pay and job requirements. I will never forget this incident. Since then, I have become very open to recognizing potential glass ceilings and working to resolve them.

Glass ceilings have been in place for hundreds of years and will likely take as long to be reversed. As new people with fresh ideas and diverse backgrounds enter the workplace, a new system will result. This is why the need for diversity training in the workplace is so important. I believe the most effective way of breaking these ceilings is to promote to our youth an appreciation for diversity and the concept that despite the gender, race, or religion of a person, we are all created equally. I have to laugh at the idea that some managers expect you to be at work, performing your job, no matter what happens in your own home; meanwhile their wives may be at home caring for their children. It's frustrating when men in the workplace don't respect your responsibilities as a businesswoman and a mother. This is a huge barrier for the working mom; sometimes you're looked at as though you have too much baggage!

While enrolled in graduate school, a professor posed a question to me regarding my perception of glass ceilings. My response to his inquiry was short and concise: "there are no glass ceilings in my world." In disbelief, many of my classmates looked at me in shock. Some even referred to my statement as idealistic. However, my life philosophy is based upon this very principle—that only I can suppress my dreams. My belief is that the very admittance of glass ceilings is a hindrance to success. Although a mere cliché, I strongly believe in my own ability to achieve the impossible. My limitations extend beyond the stars and this belief is my secret to success.

While many of my counterparts struggle with glass ceilings in their professional lives, my glass ceilings are a little more complex. My glass ceilings share more with me than just the same pot of coffee or office space-we share the same last names and DNA. With much hesitation, I confess that my glass ceilings are my family members. During my childhood years, my family was not a stable support unit; they never supported or acknowledged my interests or goals. Despite the fact that my family did provide me with the basic necessities like food, shelter, and clothing, they deprived me of emotional necessities like encouragement and positive feedback. My parents were not well-educated and as a result never motivated me to pursue my educational aspirations beyond high school. While enrolled in college, I was forced to grow up quickly—solely supporting myself financially, spiritually, and emotionally. Even to this day, when I speak of my interest in returning back to school to obtain a graduate degree, my parents act as if my desire to further my education is worse than the plague. At times, I feel like they may be intimidated about my educational achievements. If it weren't for my friends, I would have allowed my parents' negative perception of me to alter my own self-worth. Maybe the fact that my family cannot be happy for my successes is more their glass ceiling than mine, but dealing with these ongoing issues is very difficult. Glass ceilings can be an emotional deterrent to your success and your ability to excel, but only if you allow them to. I have paved a greater path for myself and I know that glass ceilings are only rocks along my journey to bigger and better destinations. In my opinion, the best way to cope with glass ceilings is to focus on the many rewards of life that God has given me—good friends, a great job, and a wonderful companion. When this coping strategy doesn't work, I don't wait until the glass ceilings hit me in the head, I just duck!

HOMAGE

"Beyond this lifetime, I desire to remain in the hearts and minds of those who I have influenced."

"Homage is not to be expected, it is to be earned. The least I could do is pay homage to those who came before me—those who have sacrificed more than I could ever imagine."

The least I could do is pay homage to those who came before me—those who have sacrificed more than I could ever imagine. I don't believe paying homage requires an elaborate event, but to simply remember and pass on the history of your family and your culture is significant. In my own family, I pay homage to my ancestors by asking questions about their life and history. While giving them an opportunity to reminisce, I let them know that I am interested in their life story.

The act of paying homage is so often displayed in the form of a salute or a bow of reverence. However, it is far more compelling than a mere way of greeting someone of high stature. While there are so many facets of life that I respect and revere, at the top of my list are the female predecessors whose hard work and diligence have paved the way for my success. These women made success an option for my generation. Their sacrifice and unduly contributions not only gave birth to generations of families, but also changed the way people perceived ambitious, outspoken, and assertive women.

When I think of these women, I think of my mother, grandmother, aunts, and cousins. I also think of those strangers whose courageous spirit and resilient aura during times of turmoil, never faltered. The heart of our nation resides within the devotion and dedication of these women. These women demanded respect, not because of their gender, but because of their ability to empower and influence. These are the women I celebrate and strive to emulate. I often reflect upon the accomplishments these women made, despite the inconceivable feats that they encountered.

I measure my success in life by my effectiveness in touching the lives of those with whom I interact. At times, I evaluate my impact by trying to imagine a world without my presence. However, just as I am in the midst of this thought, I become overwhelmed with emotion as I remember the infinite number of women whose lives I have positively influenced. At the conclusion of this daydream, I smile at the thought that someday these women will pay homage to me.

It is at this very moment that I am reassured that even if I do not live to see another day, my time on this earth has been worthwhile; I have made my contribution to society. Beyond this lifetime, I desire to remain in the hearts and minds of those that I have influenced. Homage is not to be expected, it is to be earned. Through it we ascertain the opportunity to leave a legacy that others will want to revere, respect, and remember. I think I am well on my way to scripting the words on my tombstone. What words will be on yours?

I personally don't think everybody is entitled to homage. When a person does not display respectful behavior towards others, then he or she should not expect to receive it in return. I've been used and mistreated by others throughout my life who thought their actions would gain my reverence. However, instead of gaining my respect their actions only ended up giving me more reasons to lose respect for them. We should always remain mindful about how we treat others. If we want to receive homage, we must be certain to give it. As women, it is partially our responsibility to exhibit qualities that are honorable, reputable, and thus deserving of homage. The way we carry ourselves can be a determinant in how much respect we receive.

To me, there's nothing worse in a relationship than a man who does not show homage towards his female companion or vice versa. I am a modern woman who possesses old-fashioned dating values. At an early age, my parents taught me the value of my womanhood. They also taught me that I should expect to receive respect at all times from the men I date and interact with—anything less was viewed as unacceptable. Their rationale was that if these men were reaping the benefits of my company and womanhood, then they should be willing to grant me homage in return, at the very least. During my teenager years, my parents would not allow me to leave the house with guys who did not come in to meet them prior to taking me out on a date. Furthermore, while growing up I watched my father open car doors and pull out chairs for my mother on every occasion, formal or casual. These solid examples of homage helped me build a foundation of values that validated my worth as a woman. My father always told me that I was a queen and should never settle for being treated any less than royalty. As women, we are all queens—all deserving of royal treatment and the highest regard. In many cases, if you don't demand respect from the men you interact with, then you won't receive it. Allowing your femininity to be undermined or compromised is a form of self-disrespect. Maybe you are the one who should be held accountable for the dishonorable treatment you are being rendered. If you subject yourself to disrespectful behavior, then you are partly to blame for being a recipient of it. Over the years, I have grown to appreciate receiving chivalric attention from the men I date and I enjoy it because I know I deserve it. If you are involved in a relationship that lacks homage, then maybe you need to recalculate your values and figure out how you fit into this equation that you call a relationship. Don't accept anything less than the homage you deserve!

Homage is a topic that is dear to my heart. My parents are from the South, so I was raised with virtues of respect, honor, and reverence for all people, especially those to whom it was due. I see so little of that today and feel it is desperately missing from our society. Synonymous to homage is honor and it should be rendered to whoever deserves it. With honor also comes loyalty. Loyalty is so important, especially when it relates to friendships and the student-teacher relationship. A person wants to feel that no matter what someone will be there for him or her or will be committed to him or her through thick and thin. If you've ever taken karate lessons or even watched karate, you have witnessed one of the best examples of a student-teacher relationship being displayed. No matter what level the student excels to, he or she always pays homage to the teacher. Even when the student has mastered the craft he or she still continues to exude honor, respect, and loyalty towards the teacher-it is a known fact that without the teacher he or she wouldn't be a formidable opponent.

I want my everyday life to be exemplified in such a way that 1) brings honor and glory to Jesus Christ and 2) brings total respect and reverence to those who have taught me everything I know. I pay homage to many people, especially the men and women who sacrifice their lives to protect our country—the amazing United States of America. I also pay homage to the men and women who were called to teach the word of God. Lastly, I pay homage to my family and ancestors before me who fought for the equality of women so that today, whatever I set my mind to, I can achieve!

I can vividly recall the day I met Rosa Parks. Although our meeting was brief, the impression that she had on me was a lasting one. Such a humble woman who had made a profound impact on the civil rights era, Mrs. Parks was very deserving of homage. What I learned most from my interaction with her was that it's not what you do, but instead how you do it. I wonder if Mrs. Parks ever imagined that her simple act of refusing to give up her bus seat would have resulted in such a powerful historical movement. Paying homage means uplifting those who have had an impact on your life in some way.

INTIMACY

"Trust is the main ingredient that causes an intimate relationship to grow, without it intimacy cannot flourish."

"In this day, it seems unrealistic that people will wait to engage in sexual intimacy until marriage. Marriage can take years, and intimacy is sometimes devalued in the process."

When it comes to romantic relationships, I have always been a sucker for physical intimacy. I do not like to expose my emotional side at all. Full exposure does not happen until all my boxes on the "Mr. Right" list have been checked off. Many men think because physical intimacy occurs, women automatically become emotionally involved, but for me I guess I fall in with the small percentage of women who don't get attached too easily. I feel that to some extent the physical contact does fulfill an emotional need for me. Secretly, I always thought that being too emotional was a sign of weakness; now after several years of marriage, I can cry whenever and wherever I want.

Intimacy is a personal oneness that you share with another, usually achieved through complete openness and trust. People involved in a close relationship must reach a point where there are no longer any barriers between them. Intimacy is often confused with a sexual relationship, but I have found that you can have an intimate relationship with your closest friends. Your best friends know your goals, dreams and fears—and that creates intimacy. Trust is the main ingredient that causes an intimate relationship to grow, without it intimacy cannot flourish. Common goals or shared aspirations cause individuals to connect. Intimacy continues to grow every day the relationship exists, it is ever changing and a truly intimate relationship is accepting of the change that occurs.

I would like to think it was my parents and grandparents who taught me about intimacy, but honestly I can't recall. I have always tried to model my serious relationships after my parents'. It is funny that the older you become the more your parents expose to you the more intimate details of their own relationships. Their relationship has taught me that true intimate love is tough, unyielding and always supportive of the other no matter what.

Intimacy to me means sharing the most personal parts of oneself with someone else. In romantic relationships, I believe reaching emotional intimacy will help strengthen the bond between both partners and lead to better physical intimacy. It is hard being a single woman and establishing intimacy with someone. I find it especially difficult to have physical intimacy without a relationship. The physical aspects of a relationship are so much better when emotional intimacy exists. I must admit though, it is a challenge to suppress physical desires when you aren't in a relationship with someone. At times, guilt comes into play due to my Christian beliefs about sex before marriage, but I am human too. I have felt weak at times and have tried to fight the urge. At other times I have given in to physical desires. It can be very tempting to become sexually involved with someone based on superficial attraction. In my experience, this is never is a good thing. Someone will eventually get hurt, and you don't want that someone to be you.

Once a relationship is established it takes time to build intimacy, and allowing yourself to be vulnerable is very scary. It takes both parties in the relationship to work at intimacy. One person can't do it alone. At this point in my life I would like to have someone special, but also I know it will come in due time. There is no rush. I think relationships are better when they have a chance to grow at their own pace. For right now, I am enjoying my "singlehood," free of the stresses associated with being in a relationship.

I was raised to believe that sex before or without marriage is wrong; this is a dilemma I have battled with for a long time. In this day, it seems unrealistic that people will wait to engage in sexual intimacy until marriage. Marriage can take years, and intimacy is sometimes devalued in the process. I do think every woman should find a way to demonstrate her value for sexual intimacy—whether by limiting her number of partners or by waiting until marriage. I can remember, even when I was in elementary school, having friends who had already experienced physical intimacy. I sometimes felt left out. When my mother discovered that some of the children my age were having sex, she prevented me from going to parties or sleepovers. Now that I am older, I appreciate my mother's strictness. She helped me to understand the value of intimacy. When I was younger I was shy, and felt that because of my inexperience I "was behind" everyone else. Later, when I met the love of my life, he made me feel comfortable with intimacy. I learned that intimacy with love is a gift. It is definitely something that deserves to be valued.

Even more important than sharing a physically intimate experience with someone is being emotionally intimate with him or her first. Emotional intimacy involves disclosing matters of the heart that are sometimes difficult to reveal. I can recall going for months without being physically intimate with a partner just because I wanted to enhance my emotional closeness first. Perfecting our emotional intimacy first allowed us to develop a stronger connection and therefore boosted our physical intimacy when we decided the time was right.

True intimacy is reciprocated and not unrequited. Intimacy is less physical and more about how two people relate to one another. From birth, we are introduced to one of the most important parts of intimacy—touch. It is human nature to want to be close to others. As we grow older, we never really escape that same infantile need for touch. Many people equate physical intimacy with sex. However, sex is just one of the many ways we can express intimacy.

Many people, couples especially, underestimate the power of touch. Sometimes a hug, sensual massage, kiss, cuddling, making time to talk, or simply holding hands can be more powerful than sex. In fact, if more time was spent showing these gestures, then the end result would be more sex. Intimacy adds more meaning and enjoyment to sex. In a romantic relationship, the key should be on developing a close emotional bond, but not neglecting the intellectual, social, or physical components. All components of intimacy are essential to the success of any relationship. Intimacy should be a lifestyle—acts that are so regular that they become second nature.

If you want to develop an intimate relationship, just remember the 3 T's: talk, togetherness, and touch. Establish a good foundation by communicating. You don't have to agree on everything, but you should be comfortable with sharing your thoughts, even if it is in opposition. Communicate how you feel about each other regularly. Also, try maintaining togetherness with your partner by becoming involved in activities that he or she enjoys. Plan "together" time and arrange for a sitter, if you have children. Lastly, try to incorporate more touching into your interactions. Physical interactions are very rewarding, so don't take for granted your time together with your mate. Remember to kiss one another daily, especially before leaving in the morning and going to bed at night. Try holding hands in public, giving a massage for no reason, and cuddling while watching television. Instead of sleeping on "your side of the bed," lay really close to your mate at night. Even when sex is out of the question, remember not to underestimate the value of intimacy.

JEALOUSY

"Jealousy is merely a measure of our insecurities. By disposing this negative energy, we free ourselves to become prosperous and to live life without the bars of false hope."

"I may say to myself, I wish my shape was like hers or I wish my hair could look like that. I constantly talk about it. I sometimes take it a step further and make negative comments about someone who looks great, all because of jealousy."

Jealousy is one of the most powerful emotions one can experience. It brews within one feelings of deceit and defeat. There is no end to the weight of the jealous undertones one may experience. Whether the jealousy is based upon wanting something someone possesses or an urge for someone's attention, it is unhealthy and surely a waste of time and energy. In no way will being jealous or envious of others allow us to prosper. When we become jealous of others, we begin to lose sight of our purpose in life. Jealousy is merely a measure of our insecurities. By disposing this negative energy, we free ourselves to become prosperous. Only through this option will we truly experience serenity and prosperity.

I believe jealousy can be a positive emotion. Jealousy can be the fuel necessary to help you aspire to achieve bigger and better things. For example, as a child I would see successful individuals and would try to model myself after them. The first emotion I felt was jealousy, followed by a sense of admiration. Jealousy allowed me to recognize a hidden desire within myself. Feelings of jealousy creep into my mind every day. Whether in the form of admiring something a person possesses or realizing that someone makes more money than I do, it isn't difficult for me to realize that jealousy plays an active role in my life. To counteract these emotions, I try to direct my energy to positive things. I don't want negative feelings of jealousy to consume me!

Negative energy, such as jealousy can and does pose a great big obstacle when trying to reach a particular goal. Steering clear of people who don't possess goals that are similar to your own is the best thing to do. Women that encourage other women in relationships to leave their mates over trivial matters should be watched very carefully. You must first consider their motive and rationale. Women should surround themselves with other women who aspire to see one another achieve the very best. Eliminating the jealousy can eliminate simple obstacles in your own path.

I believe jealousy is more accepted within romantic relationships because people tend to confuse jealously with love. When jealousy exists in a relationship, the love between people is fueled by the energy that jealousy brings … and when that jealousy is no longer present, the relationship is bound to erode.

I would like to think that I don't have a jealous bone in my body, but that is not the case. Some may argue that feelings of jealousy could be a positive thing. I don't agree. I have had jealous feelings when I see a nice looking person or someone that dresses nicely. I may say to myself, I wish my shape was like hers or I wish my hair could look like that. I constantly talk about it. I sometimes take it a step further and make negative comments about someone who looks great all because of jealousy. There have been times when I have caught myself thinking "why can't that be me?" or "why can't my husband do those things for me?" At this point, I have not confronted or controlled these feelings as much as I would like to. I guess I am not totally happy with my current situation or myself. This problem can't be rectified until I confront my own issues. The bottom-line is that we need self-love. I think you first have to love yourself in order to appreciate when someone else is doing well.

Jealousy is not a four-letter-word! Anger and grief both get respect. Love is revered. Yet, jealousy is denied and besmirched. Most people feel jealousy at some point in their lives for a variety of reasons, but nobody wants to admit to it. I believe all emotions have a purpose in our lives and jealousy just gets a bad rap. *Any* emotion can turn into something negative when the emotion is misplaced or excessive. On the other hand, if we acknowledge and seek to understand our emotions we can put all of them to good use.

Why does society feel that anger is sometimes justified but jealousy never is? I believe it is because jealousy reveals our deepest insecurities … and few people want to show people their greatest weakness. If I, as a single woman, feel jealous when I see a couple and their child is that so awful? Does feeling jealous mean that I am unhappy, selfish, or mean? Am I supposed to feel ashamed? No, this feeling simply means that I would like to meet someone and someday start a family of my own. I think jealousy is harmful only when it moves beyond feeling a desire for something you see, to having negative thoughts towards people who possess what you desire. Just as anger can have the positive effect of pushing you to take action against an injustice or to overcome an obstacle, jealousy can help you understand your true desires and move you to set positive goals to find fulfillment. No emotion is bad, it's all in the way you manifest them!

Jealousy is a sneaky emotion that creeps up when you are not expecting it. Its roots lie within our insecurities. But what do you do when that green-eyed monster creeps up on you? Jealousy waltzes into the workplace environment with high heels and a subtle confidence that makes you wonder "What's so special about her?" If you don't catch it, the emotion of jealousy can turn into anger and resentment. The green-eyed monster can make us doubt ourselves and wonder "What's wrong with me?" It is especially important for women to kill the monster of jealously before it takes control of our lives, emotions, and careers. We must slaughter the monster, so we can work together. We must practice avoiding the monster, so we can learn from each other's mistakes. Most importantly, we must murder the monster of jealousy, so we can share in our sisters' joys, sorrows, and rejoice in the spirit of sisterhood.

I saw the way you looked at me when I shared with you my dreams and aspirations, but I couldn't understand why. I tried to contact you to share with you the exciting news about my new job, but you never returned my call—I couldn't understand why. We're good friends, so I know it's not possible for you to be envious of me, right? Well if this is the case, then why do I smell the aroma of jealousy brewing? Is it possible that you are envious of my success? Why would you resent me when you have had the same opportunities to excel as I? Could it be that you are using me as a scapegoat for your disappointments? While you were chasing fast cars, I was being chased by adversity. While you were watching cars cruise by, I was cruising around mountains of glass ceilings. Yes, it is true that I have worked hard to get to success avenue; it has been a long drive. However, I realize that I cannot sit back and allow others to drive my car while I am sitting in the passenger seat. I must put my car into first gear and avoid braking until my goal is accomplished. In my drive to success, I have watched many acquaintances become jealous of my ambitions and my achievements. Before you began harboring jealous feelings because of the success another is experiencing, you should stop and take a good look at yourself. Examine first the wrong turns you have made in your life, then take action and get back on the right road. Don't hold anyone, except for yourself accountable for your shortcomings and certainly don't use jealousy as a mechanism to propel you to greater heights. Remember, what God has done for others, he can do for you. When you can genuinely be happy for the success others are experiencing, you are ready to reap your own success. Start manifesting positive energy and in due time you will yield positive results.

KINDRED

"Grandparents shape our parents, our parents shape us, and there are a host of aunts, uncles and cousins that have a role in making us who we are or become."

"The family's role is to instill values, build character, and give guidance."

My mother is my best friend because she has always been there for me. Although she had me at a young age, she did an excellent job of raising me. She could have easily given me up but she didn't. With the help of my grandmother, my mom was able to graduate from high school, go on to college and attain a degree. As soon as she finished, she came and got me. We've been together since then. We always had a decent place to stay and food was always provided. Not once did my mom expose me to dangerous environments; I never lacked anything. On the other hand, I am working hard to strengthen my relationship with my father because he was not part of my life as I was growing up. We both have been working on rebuilding the relationship. It has not been easy, but I see progress. It may never get to the level we both desire. However, it's better than before, and we're still trying. Life is too short to hold grudges. It just feels good when you have a healthy, solid, close relationship with your family. You look forward to every gathering with them.

The role of the family is to guide its individual members on the right path. People intrinsically believe that family should support you no matter what the circumstance. This can also be a sticky situation; supporting an individual when he or she is wrong does a disservice to that individual and to anyone else who may be affected by his or her actions. This also includes turning a blind eye to things that should not be tolerated. Family can be your biggest critic or your number one fan. The family shapes morality, or our view of life, and that is why it is very important that we as individuals take our roles in the family seriously.

Family has influenced everything in my life: from the college I attended, the way I practice my faith, the man I married, and the way I raise my son. Grandparents shape our parents, our parents shape us, and there are a host of aunts, uncles and cousins that have a role in making us who we are or become. I try to show my son that I love him, not only by saying it, but also through my actions. I will pass on family traditions and teach him that he can be whatever he wants as long as he is willing to work hard at it.

Families are the first line of defense for every child. They should serve as protectors, teachers, and providers. Most families strive to be all of these things to their children. Unfortunately, many are unable to adequately meet all of these needs. The family's role as a protector is to shield children from the ill-wills of society. Although this is something that cannot be controlled, it is the family's responsibility to minimize a defenseless child's exposure to harm. The family's role is to instill values and responsibility, build character, and give guidance. Most families pass on both the good and bad lessons that they were taught. Through these lessons, the child eventually learns what it means to be a responsible adult and provide for their future families.

Every child has basic needs that must be nourished in order to grow and flourish. The family's role as provider is to meet the basic needs of their children and, when possible, go beyond. The challenge for most parents is to help their children distinguish wants from needs.

A great friendship with my mother is something I strive for. There have been times in my life when I don't feel that she has been there for me. There is nothing that compares to a daughter feeling that her mother doesn't support her. Our relationship has gotten a lot better, but it still has miles to go. I want our relationship to be one that can be modeled by my daughter, if I have one some day.

Friends may come and go, but the foundation of a family is the infrastructure of our society. I place a great deal of emphasis on maintaining healthy relationships with all of my family members. However, over the years one relationship stands out in my mind—the relationship I have with my father. My father and I have overcome many obstacles in our relationship, most of which seem to emanate from different life philosophies. Nevertheless, with God's guidance we have been able to sweep these differences under the rug to reconcile a relationship that was once faltered.

The role of a family is to be supportive. When no one else is there for you, your family should be. Family members should display love unconditionally. When I think about my family, a dysfunctional unit comes to mind. A family should be a cohesive unit, but this is not the case. In most cases, things are negative; even the most positive interactions can become negative. This behavior originated with past generations and continues to manifest even now. The healthy relationships in my life are with my cousins. We have all watched our parents' relationships deteriorate as they continue to treat each other like strangers. We have vowed to break the cycle of negativity by moving forward fostering only positive behaviors. I think we have been able to overcome obstacles by continuing to maintain open communication; everyone respects one another's ideas and opinions. Respect is the key because without it one might begin to speak malicious words. This would cause conflict and lead to hurt feelings and possible resentment. When our parents are at odds, we do our best to remain neutral. By remaining neutral we can ensure that the lines of communication are not distorted. We must continue striving to set positive examples of kindred love for our children and future generations to come.

The common denominator in the word kindred is similarity. Kindred can be referenced through my relationships with family or through my association with persons based upon our similarities in beliefs, qualities, or our attitudes towards a situation. The reason I am most familiar with this meaning is because my family is small and I have therefore always had friends who were just like my family. As a matter of fact, they *are* family. I have been able to maintain close relationships with my friends for 5, 10, and as much as 20 years because of the strong moral values we share in common. We have chosen to take many different career paths in life such as entrepreneurship, teaching, sales, etc. However, through all the changes something remains constant, and that is making good, solid, and morally sound decisions. This quality couldn't be traded for anything in the world because when the dust settles, we will always be kindred spirits.

Poetic Interlude
"The Prosperity Principle"

What if we experienced this world
From a completely different perspective?
A different point of view?

It may seem quite strange,
As new things often do.
No more glass half empty,
Just glass half full;
And all that seemed impossible
Looks very promising to you!

What if the world was really meant
To be set up for bliss?
For everybody to be happy loving,
And let's add Prosperity to this list.

There would be no more bad luck,
Black clouds, you get my drift?
Why Murphy's Law would be viewed as
An outrageous, preposterous myth!

So without smashing your tomatoes,
Just simply changing the old,

Let's adopt a new way of thinking,
"Prosperity Principle".... SOLD!

© 2004 Written by the late Tracy "Imani" Lynne Davis

PART II

❀

LIFE'S PERSPECTIVES FROM L–Z

LIBERATION

"What right does one have to deprive you of your personal interests and views—even if he is your husband? Who wants to live life without full liberation?"

"I wanted to be accepted. Then I said STOP! Why are you searching for their approval? I had to teach myself how to love and appreciate myself and believe it."

My definition of liberation is being set free from conforming to others' actions and beliefs. My most liberating experience has been to let go of what people think of me. In the past, I have valued how others perceived me, and when their ideas and thoughts of me were negative, I worked hard to change their minds. I wanted to be accepted. I realized that I had to teach myself how to love and appreciate myself and believe it. Once this was done, I felt inner peace.

When you can let people go, peace will flow through your life. Peace simply means the absence of war. The wars that you have with people and the inner wars you have with yourself can be put to rest or at least be harmonious. This liberation has strengthened my character because I am now an independent thinker and others seek my opinion and value my thoughts. I would never have experienced this if I would have continued to be held captive by my fears of rejection and anger. For those of you that seek liberty for yourself remember to confront your fears, release negative thoughts, and become an independent thinker.

In order to reach a level of full liberation, a woman must totally free herself of all inhibitions, including those which may emanate from what others may think, say, or feel about her. As a married woman who frequently makes decisions that do not coincide with my husband's views, I struggle with the idea of conforming to traditional wife roles. After watching so many once self-sufficient and independent women succumb to their husband's power, only to become the second rate spouse, I am skeptical of relinquishing too much of my liberation. When I exert my liberation, I am accused of being an individualistic and selfish partner. However, my belief is that my husband's discomfort with my liberation is his own issue. At times, I wonder if being single has greater benefits than being married. It seems to me that being a single woman means being free of all encumbrances. What right does one have to deprive you of your personal interests and views—even if he is your husband, boyfriend, or a supervisor at work? Who wants to live life without full liberation? I refuse to do so and so should you!

Personal liberation is about freeing your soul from those ties that bind you. Most difficult is liberating oneself from those ties that are created by the people we're close to and things we desire. Perhaps you need to liberate yourself from the comfort of the warm body lying beside you, the material possessions you work so hard for, or that steady (but unrewarding) job. How many people really love the thought of giving these things up? At first, untying yourself may feel more like you're just unraveling! This year I moved from my hometown to a new city, and for me the physical relocation was also surprisingly liberating. Living outside of my comfort zone helped me find my own rhythm. I found that being in a place that I was fairly unfamiliar with and knew only a few people brought about unexpected changes in the way I did things. I thought I was independent before, but realized there were so many things I took for granted that I now had to put thought into. At home everything I needed was pretty much in place, while now I am creating my own way. I guess liberation is sometimes a by-product of the little choices we make. I am convinced that if you physically remove yourself from whatever holds you back emotionally, your mind will soon find liberation. The more we take the chance to open ourselves to new challenges, the more likely we are to find personal freedom.

The liberation I seek is different I surmise, from that sought by most women my age. While it seems most of the women I interact with are seeking a mate to help them experience fulfillment, I am seeking to liberate myself from this ideal. Society has done a great job of convincing women that they can only experience true happiness if they are involved in a relationship that will lead to marriage. Sometimes, I don't feel like marriage is a part of my destiny, not because it's not an option, but because I think it will counteract my freedom. There is a side of me that really enjoys companionship of the opposite sex, but the other side of me wants to be free to live life through my own binoculars. I am very realistic about my future and realize that marriage may not be a part of my script. This thought makes me happy, not because I don't want to ever experience the joy of being married, but because I don't want to feel like my life cannot be fulfilling without it. I don't want to regret later in life not enjoying the freedom of my singlehood today. I enjoy being single and being free. I enjoy being liberated!

Stop running up and down the steps … please sit down and stay seated … finish your homework! I love my child, but sometimes I feel like I need to escape the ongoing duties I inherited through parenthood. At times, I feel parenthood is more of a punishment, than a benefit; I feel trapped and confined. When I first got married, everyone encouraged me to bear offspring, but no one ever told me that I would be sacrificing every ounce of my freedom. Every now and then, mothers need to be granted liberation from their duly responsibilities. Since we are the givers of life, we have earned the right to enjoy the liberation that life gives us!

MONEY

"Money gives me the energy I need to keep working until I reach the top ... and at the top is more money."

"I believe there is something money cannot buy and that is "LOVE." Love should come from the heart."

Money has been a primary motivator in my decision to pursue a career in sales and to start my own business. However, there are just some things that I wouldn't do for money. My belief is that we all should walk in integrity, and be in remembrance of the Golden Rule, do unto others, as you'd have them do unto you. I actually do believe that the love of money is the root of evil. The way in which one handles his or her money is just an indication of that individual's morals. If a person has a good heart and good moral intentions, then that will be exemplified in some of their financial choices. On the contrary, if a person doesn't have good intentions or good moral values, then their financial decisions will usually reflect these same standards.

Money is definitely being used in our society as a measure of an individual's success. The more money one has, the higher quality of goods and services one can obtain. In our society, if people have money, or appear to have money, it seems as if they have "arrived," and are treated as such. However, we really and truly don't have personal freedom until we have economic freedom. That just simply means being totally debt free and to owe no man anything but love. I most definitely believe the world could revolve without money, but only on one premise…. that there is some other form of exchange for goods and services. If bananas were the common denominator for the exchange of goods and services, then we would all have bananas. If it were rocks, then we would all use rocks. For now, money is what our society has chosen for the common denominator. So, until further notice, this is what we will have to use if we want to continue receiving goods and services.

Money to me is important, but it is not everything. The only worry I have regarding money is that I will not have enough to live and enjoy the special aspects of life. I would like to maximize my earning potential, but I am not motivated by money. My belief is that headaches generally escort professional positions that pay higher salaries. I want to obtain balance in life. I believe to whom much is given, much is expected. I try to practice good financial habits. In fact, I am currently working on becoming debt free and plan to accomplish this goal later next year. Additionally, although I am decades away from retirement, I am constantly planning for my future by investing my money. However, at times, I do feel the need to splurge a bit. I take annual vacations and dine out regularly.

I sincerely believe that when you worship an idol of any kind, you are sinning against GOD. In today's society, many people put money ahead of all other concerns. It is what drives them. Many feel their identities are measured by how much money they make. However, I feel a major part of my success is determined by how I treat others and live my life. Money comes and goes; it is not more important than my family and friends. They don't come and go. I would love to be comfortable and not live from paycheck to paycheck, but when I get to that point it be enough? I think so, because all that really matters to me in the end anyway is my health, my family, and my friends.

Believe it or not, my personal definition of wealth does not even include the word money. Although I am cognizant that this possession is necessary in order to function in our society, I do not condone the transformation of one's values for it. I hear so many people say they'd do anything for money. Just today, I watched a lovely married couple gulp down one gallon of wiggling worms just to claim a measly $10,000. Have things become so financially disastrous that people are willing to spare their dignity, not to mention their digestive tracts just for money? Talking about a sacrifice of integrity ... the episode continued with another couple waddling in pig's blood and taking a dip in below zero degree water just to prove one solid point—that their love for money had gone beyond reason. Needless to say, it is not their fault that they have fallen victim to society's "love of money syndrome." Their infatuation with the dollar bill has only been perpetuated by the airing of endless daredevil reality shows whose mission is to test how far people will go to win money … week after week contestants on reality shows perform outrageous stunts that demonstrate how eager some people are to forego their dignity on national television just to ascertain wealth. My belief is that by allowing money to control your life, you are allowing man to guide your destiny. When this is the case, you are no longer putting your faith in God, but instead placing it in worldly possessions. The value of life should not be measured by what man deems important or successful. Instead, it should be measured by our investment in our personal stocks—those that cannot be sold, traded, or lose value on the NASDAQ, namely our families and friends.

Money is very important to me. Without it, I feel insecure and worthless. Most of my life's goals and dreams are based upon my desire to make money. My decision to attend college was primarily fueled by my desire to make money. I have had a lot of challenges in my life. Each job change and promotion has been for the need of "more money." I am still searching for a different job with my company for the want of "more money." I will continue to search and climb up this corporate ladder to provide for my child's needs and wants. Money gives me the drive and energy I need to continue to tolerate "a job." Money gives me the opportunity to dream … dream about all that life has to offer. Unfortunately, money is very important in my life. Without it, I will think that I have failed my life and daughter. I say "unfortunately" because to some, it is sad to say that money weighs so heavily in a person's life. But if they would look at what money allows, maybe the importance of money would be better understood. I believe there is something money cannot buy and that is "LOVE." Love should come from the heart. Money is very important. I love it. I need it. Money gives me the energy I need to keep working until I reach the top … and at the top is more money.

NAIVETY

"As you go through life and experience different situations, your naivety for those situations will diminish."

"The mistakes I have made should teach me lessons, but naivety always shows up to the rescue."

Yes, I admit that I sometimes demonstrate naïve behavior. Especially in my younger years naivety was surely one of my areas of weakness. In relationships, it took me a while to realize when I was being manipulated. When I was involved with someone, they captured my total trust. Working in the human service field has really helped me become more aware of this weakness. I have grown completely out of this mindset and have now become cognizant that although I wish to see the best in a person, their intentions may not be genuine in nature. I am not sure if I have become less naïve because I have matured mentally or acquired more meaningful life experiences. I can only guess that it must be a combination of both factors. I believe a person can overcome naïve tendencies by gaining more insight through open forums, support groups, and guidance from friends, family members, and education.

The older I grow, the more realistic my views of the world become. However, I still feel I am naïve about people to a certain degree. Although, I know that people are capable of any and everything I do hope and do try to look for the best in people. I sometimes give people more credit and more chances than they deserve, especially in relationships. I have a habit of getting "caught up" in situations, especially when I really like the person. On many occasions, I have ignored the warning signs of relationships because I construed their actions as a sign that they were seriously interested in me. I have lost count of the number of times I have gone out on dates thinking that the relationship was going to endure, but never even received a phone call from the person. The mistakes I have made, should teach me lessons, but naivety always shows up to the rescue. I realize that I must make a conscious decision to overcome naivety by being open to learning about myself and understanding the mistakes that I have made. Only when those situations arise again and I rectify my way of dealing with them, will I be able to say that I am no longer naïve. As you go through life and experience different situations, your naivety for those situations will diminish.

Naivety is a microcosm of society. Everyday, we face societal dilemmas that support this ideal. One of the most detrimental forms of naivety is the HIV epidemic. There are so many who have been affected by this plague and the sole reason for this skyrocketing effect is naivety. People are becoming infected with this virus at an escalating rate. My belief is that education is the only key to unlocking the door of naivety. By creating and maintaining a platform on which we can discuss issues that are imperative to our society, we can eradicate naivety. Only through naivety can a pandemic of this magnitude continue to exist. It is time that we all get clear about the issues of HIV and spread the word for further prevention.

Naivety isn't always a negative quality. Sometimes being naïve can be a strategy. People are far less likely to view a woman as a threat when she assumes a naïve persona. True wisdom is knowing when to display a certain characteristic at the right time, especially when dating. The people who call me naïve should really be calling me insightful. It takes a brilliant woman to know which cards she should play at the right time.

Growing up with a lineage of positive women role models who always protected me from harm, I was sheltered from a lot of life's experiences. Even now at the age of 31, I still feel that I'm naïve about many aspects of life. When it comes to certain topics, some of my acquaintances perceive me as being aloof and oblivious. To some degree, I believe my naivety has helped me to maintain a positive outlook on life. I have purposefully sheltered myself from the harsh realities of life by pretending that they don't exist. However, when I come off of my cloud, I realize the reality of reality—that life's experiences whether good, bad, or indifferent are worth treasuring. Naivety should not prevent us from recognizing that life isn't always going to be full of positive experiences. We must begin to appreciate the wisdom that we gain from our experiences; only then will we be able to counteract our naivety.

About 14 years ago, my face would have been in the dictionary next to naïve. What's sad is that during that time, I thought I was mature and in control of everything. Sure, I knew I still had more to learn, but I thought I was taking it all in good stride-boy, was I ever wrong! I lacked experience in relationships—socially and professionally. I trusted people too easily and wanted to believe that everyone was always being upfront and honest with me. In several situations, my trustworthiness was taken advantage of. However, the best thing about being naïve is that you can overcome it. Through my experiences, I learned so much about myself, others, and the world. I wouldn't trade any of the embarrassments, tears, or the lessons I learned during my "naïve years." I am a firm believer that we evolve into a "better self" through life experiences. We go through life and if we are smart, we learn from our experiences. I don't think of bad experiences as mistakes. I think that we make choices that have unpleasant consequences. When people perceive you as naïve, it is likely that they will try to take advantage of you, but you can outgrow it! You can overcome it! Unfortunately, outgrowing and overcoming naivety is only achieved by having more experiences. You have to be critical of yourself and examine your choices when the outcome is unfavorable. In particular, you must examine your role in the outcome, along with what you learned from it. You can't live in a shell or be afraid to try new things. We are like flowers—the only way to grow is to get wet. So, I say to you "let it rain!"

OPTIMISM

"Contrary to what many believe, optimism isn't a point of view, it is a way of life."

"Even life's most dreadful encounters can be transformed with just a touch of optimism."

In the past, I would have classified myself as an eternal optimist but I now prefer to call myself a realist with optimistic tendencies. I definitely look on the bright side of circumstances and with a realistic mindset believe the best outcome will occur. Through my experiences I have discovered that it is best to be realistic. I have also learned that being optimistic opens one up for wishful thinking and pure fantasy; optimism does not necessarily mean good will come from a situation and it does not infer acceptance. In my experience, hoping for the best outcome has given way to fantasy and unrealistic expectations. Instead of just hoping for the best whatever that may be, my optimism would allow me to believe that anything was possible, which morphed into unrealistic hopes that had less than a 1% chance of actually occurring.

At times, my expectation for the best was so high that I often found myself disappointed with the outcome or forcing myself to try and make the best of a less than spectacular reality. As a result, I have learned to still see the good in things, while maintaining expectations for the best, but from a more realistic perspective. As a child, I always believed my positive energy would force goodness to occur. I have since learned that one's optimistic views will not necessarily foster good fortune. There are other times when it appears that optimism does influence the outcome of a situation.

While my father was battling cancer, I witnessed how his optimistic outlook caused him to become disappointed time and time again. The positive energy that I believed would help sustain life, proved to be non-beneficial. Up until the moment of his demise, he saw the brighter side of his situation, but in the end I am not sure that being optimistic was worth it. There are many times when I equate my optimism with acceptance. Sometimes my being optimistic is like a mask. I try to convince myself that everything happens for the best, but don't always know that this is the case. Preferring to see the good in any situation has allowed me to experience temporary comfort, but this has always led to my complacency and acceptance. At times, being optimistic has caused me to

miss opportunities because instead of asserting my dissent for the situation, I simply accepted the circumstance and assumed everything was
for the best. I have since realized that I can be optimistic without having
to sacrifice my point of view.

One chooses to perceive life's experiences from a negative or positive
outlook. Personally, I elect to view life in an optimist manner. Contrary,
to what many believe, optimism isn't a point of view, it is a way of life.
While many invest their energies into idle complaints, they have failed
to see their life as a whole picture. Additionally, they have failed to realize that the perspective they have assumed has caused them more pain
than pleasure. The results are usually seen in the form of ailing health
and high stress levels. In life there are simply matters that are beyond
our control. With this being the case, we are fighting a losing battle to
see things with the glass half empty. Our lives are only a testament of the
challenges we are able to conquer. Thus, our outlook determines the
degree in which we can combat these challenges. Optimism ensures us
that there will be another bright day and that those days that are dark
will be bright again. No matter what the circumstance, it can be viewed
optimistically. Even life's most dreadful encounters can be transformed
with just a touch of optimism. After facing numerous dilemmas, I can
personally attest to the importance of this attribute. However, I cannot
pretend as if I was born with this trait. I have been blessed to acquire this
outlook from my mother whose strength has given me the power to
share this gift with others. Although I view myself as an optimist, I also
view myself as a realist. I do not allow optimism to counteract the truth.
I firmly believe the only way to deal with a problem is to analyze the true
issue. After verifying the issue that exists, I proceed with a method that
is constructive, not destructive. The solutions to most of our daily
dilemmas reside within us. It is our responsibility to locate them!

Optimism is a state of mind, an act of faith, a positive attitude.… I only consider myself to be optimistic in the areas of my life that I have confidence in. My optimism is steadily growing day by day. I believe that one can only be termed an optimist if he or she works in a positive light and expects the best possible outcome. I am an optimist at times, especially when I have given my all to a situation. For some, when they have worked in the optimistic realm and their plan fails, they give up. This is not the best way to approach the situation. An optimist always has a plan A, B, or C and all outcomes are hopeful. However, optimism without reality can become a hindrance. Some of us do not have common sense when it comes to relationships, money, etc. We are optimistic about our financial future, but do not take the necessary steps to increase our wealth and minimize our debts. We also want our relationships to work, but refuse to put the necessary energy into making them successful. So yes, optimism can fail us, especially when we fail it. We fail it by not being true to its meaning. An optimist is wise. I am optimistic about my future … my life will be opulent in every area, but I still realize that my thoughts will not solely come to life. I am responsible for making my optimistic views a reality. I imagine a day when I can work fully in optimism and not doubt myself. Self-confidence is a very important part of being optimistic. Additionally, realizing and acknowledging your personal attributes can also be a sign of optimism.

It is so healthy to live with optimism. Doubt brings about fear and desperation. These feelings can bring an onset of illnesses and depression. We all know someone who is extremely negative and miserable. They probably aren't operating in optimism, but are instead lacking hope and faith. It is my charge to you to live with optimism, using a mixture of faith, self-confidence, and REALITY. This solution will bring about a life full of positive energy—an energy that will exude to others and make your presence appreciated by all.

It's difficult for me to fathom how people who encounter negative experiences can really maintain an optimistic attitude. I think being optimistic when dealing with dilemmas, especially those that involve tragedy, is very unrealistic and naïve. When I face challenges, I try to maintain a realistic outlook. This helps me to stay focused on finding a solution to my problem, instead of pretending like everything is okay, when it's not.

I'm not always optimistic about my life in general. However, I am optimistic that I will someday find true love and have a family. Despite the negative images that the media depicts, which emphasize the paucity of eligible educated and professional bachelors, I am confident that my soul mate awaits me. I will remain steadfast and optimistic. I will not raise my white flag to surrender until I am victorious!

PERSEVERANCE

"And just when I thought my gift was to persevere through the storm safely, my boyfriend surprised me with a marriage proposal! I said YES!"

"Perseverance means moving past failure to achieve what some may consider to be the impossible."

As I ran by, crowds of people from all walks of life embraced my presence through shouts of encouragement and support. Although they could not personally relate to my circumstance, they could relate to my hard work and struggle to accomplish my ultimate goal at the time, which was reaching the finish line. Running the race was not easy, but with the constant inspiration of strangers who I had only met minutes before the race, I was able to persevere. It became so evident to me that what mattered most was not whether I knew the names of those running along with me, but that we were all bonded together by our connection to this event. Only minutes before the pain from my legs had transformed into agony, the hand of a kind gentleman, whose name I can barely recall, was extended to me. From that point on until the conclusion of the race, this gentleman's source of strength and support became so crucial to me. Now almost three years later, feelings of emotion and graciousness still continue to engulf my mind as I recall an enduring memory—the time when the faith a stranger had in my ability to persevere, inspired me to accomplish my goal of running the New York Marathon. I often think of that stranger and wonder if he ever knew how much his compassionate heart inspired me to persevere. For it was through his faith in me that I was able to finish the race.

As the news reporter completed the weather report, I was reminded that the storm headed my way was the same storm that had devastated Grenada and Jamaica only one week prior to its visit in my hometown. As I relive those personal accounts of the storm's visit, I recap the fear I felt on that rainy night in September only one day before my 30th birthday. This was supposed to be one of the happiest days of my life—my transition into the thirty something womanhood I'd heard others speak so candidly about. Instead it was a night filled with heavy rain and winds thrashing at my window. My eyes stayed glued to the television as my boyfriend created a temporary bed out in the hallway. As time went on, the wind grew even stronger, but the eye of the storm was not expected to hit until early in the morning-just a mere two hours into my birthday. My fear only exacerbated as I continued to watch the news and learn of how quickly the storm would be arriving.

The rain continued to beat against our windows, but I still couldn't move, until the power went out! It was pitch black and we only had one flashlight and a hand full of candles. I finally went out into the hallway with my boyfriend and prayed that the storm wouldn't be too bad, but it was difficult for me to fall asleep. My heart pounded as if it were going to jump out of my chest as the wind howled like a wolf. In the midst of the storm in complete darkness, my boyfriend in a sweet and genuine gesture wished me a Happy Birthday. However, with the circumstances at hand my birthday was no longer a matter of concern. I was instead praying that I would see my birthday for a full 24 hours. As I began to hear car alarms sound around my neighborhood, I began to realize that the storm had hit. Fully in panic mode, I thought about how the storm must have been devouring the cars outside. Each minute felt like an hour. I watched the water from outside come pouring in from under the front door, but knew that this was only a sampling of what was to come. I then heard a loud crash come from the apartment above us. It sounded like the shattering of a window with the sound of heavy raindrops that followed. Smoke detectors and car alarms continued to sound in the midst of it all. As I continued to hear the heavy debris flying outside, I told myself to get rid of the negative thoughts brewing within. As hard as I tried it was extremely difficult. The next morning, I awakened to a fresh start.

As I surveyed the apartment, I noticed that by the grace of God there was no major damage. Unfortunately, that was not true for many of our neighbors. Trees were down everywhere. Some snapped in two, others completely uprooted. Debris littered the roads making them impassable. Power lines were down and traffic lights had vanished. These haunting images of Hurricane Ivan remind me everyday of how blessed I was to persevere through the storm. For it was at that very moment that I remembered it was my birthday—not the horrible one I had thought it was going to be, but the best birthday ever. I had never been so grateful to be alive. And just when I thought my gift was to get through the storm safely, my boyfriend surprised me with a marriage proposal. I said YES! As they say, perseverance has its rewards.

Perseverance is not giving up on anything you set out to do. How do I cope with the obstacles that I've faced in life thus far? I always pray for a way to get pass, through, over or around my obstacles. I sometimes find it difficult to move forward following obstacles. My advice is that you look to your spiritual source for the strength to persevere. For me, this technique has been very effective. I depend tremendously on a healthy spiritual life. I believe perseverance is an essential component for those who wish to be successful. Many successful people have failed at tasks before finding their niche. The key is to not allow your failures to hinder your successes. Perseverance means moving past failure to achieve what some may consider to be the impossible.

We all have endured some type of obstacle in life. I feel that God allows each of us to experience different trials and tribulations based upon our strengths. My college days were a test of perseverance. I was over 10 hours away from my mom. In addition, we had what I would call a "strained relationship." My father and mother got divorced when I entered college. I guess there was not a need anymore for them to stay together since I was out of the house officially. Each wanted me to take their side, which soon became a major stressor to me. My performance in school took a major toll, but I realized that I had to think of myself. My parents had lived their lives and I was beginning to live mine. When I made this decision, my mother was unhappy. She wanted me to move to Ohio and be far away from my dad as possible. As a result, I have not spoken to my mother in over seven years. Over the years, I have grown up alone; sexually, mentally, and physically. I learned through trial and error that you can't trust everyone. You must guard your heart and body. Although, I went through college without the guidance and love of a mother, it molded me into the strong woman that I am today. With God's help, I persevered and overcame it all.

Marriage has been one of the most challenging life experiences that I have ever encountered. The ups and downs of this bumpy amusement park ride have at times made me nauseous. Along my journey through Marriageville, there were times when I didn't think I could endure, but God knew differently. He faxed my heart a memorandum reminding me of how blessed I really am—an epiphany was the result of this transmittal. It was at that very moment that I realized that my marriage was a part of God's lesson for me—that we must persevere to claim the pot of gold that awaits us at the end of life's rainbow. I am happy to say that with the assistance of a strong prescription of perseverance, the bumps and bruises in my marriage have finally healed. I am now more appreciative than ever of the lessons that were learned and the marital relationship that was strengthened in the process. When we persevere and wait patiently for God's blueprint to unfold, we can better appreciate the beauty of his masterpiece.

QUIESCENCE

"Quiet time is essential to your emotional well-being."

"Meditation is a vital element of spiritual development."

I obtain quiescence by creating order in my life. I pride myself on being very organized and believe that everyone should maintain a daily running list of "things to do." This can be very helpful in making sure that you are concentrating on your goals and focusing on your priorities. I especially feel accomplishment at the end of the day, after I can cross off the tasks I have completed. It is so exhilarating for me to feel self-sufficient and that my most valuable treasure—my time, has not been wasted. Although I put a great deal of energy into maintaining an organized disposition, I must be honest. I do not take the time to meditate like I should, but I do believe meditation is a vital part of creating a sense of peace in one's life. One of the things I love the most that helps me relax and unwind is to have an hour-long massage. I also take time to enjoy nature. I especially find relaxing inhaling the fresh and crisp air of the fall. This allows me to commune with God. Another way in which I achieve quiescence is by taking a relaxing bath. This allows me to escape to my own personal spa for a few minutes without any interruptions. Afterwards, I feel wonderfully refreshed!

I definitely feel quiet time is essential to my emotional well-being. In my profession, I am constantly working with people all day. Thus, when I have the opportunity to have self-time, I take advantage of it. I make time for myself at least once or twice per week and I still don't feel like this is sufficient. However, as an independent woman with numerous duties, I do not truly believe I will have the self-time I deserve until I am totally financially free. Until then, I will be forced to succumb to all of the daily responsibilities, but I am glad to say that I am in the process of making this happen for myself. When this occurs, I will then know the true meaning of quiescence. In conclusion, my belief is that you will never be able to get in touch with yourself or realize what God has called you to be, if you don't make time for yourself. I believe strongly that meditation is a vital element of spiritual development. It allows you not just a chance to speak with God, but more importantly, to listen to God!

I try to create order in my life by organizing my weekly schedule and organizing my home. Doing both activities helps to reduce the clutter in my life. As a means to acquire quiescence, I meditate on occasions, but have not yet incorporated this practice into my daily regimen. Recently, in an attempt to reduce distress in my life, I have developed an interest in pilates and yoga. Currently, I employ breathing exercises, spiritual reading, and create a spa-like environment in my home using bath and candles, which allow me to relax.

As a professional woman with a very demanding job, it is easy to become overwhelmed with a fast paced and jam packed work schedule. Although it is very challenging to combat stress, I make it my priority to find quiet time. Whether, making time to get a professional massage, get my hair done, or read a book, I realize the importance of a tranquil lifestyle and surely take advantage of it. While my goal is to exercise at least 2–3 days a week, I sometimes become preoccupied with other household chores. If I am unable to make the necessary self-time throughout the week, then I plan "down time" during the weekend. Life's too short, I'm going to enjoy it while I can!

Our society places too much emphasis on the *passing* of time.... so much that we lose sight of the *presence* of time. As a female, I think there is a greater pressure to juggle multiple priorities. We make time for family, friends, work, school, church and everything else. In a society where being busy is worn as a badge of honor, I think many women unfortunately feel guilty for stepping away from daily tasks to focus on their inner selves. Seeking serenity is a "guilty pleasure" I encourage all women to indulge in!

When you wake up in the morning and hit that snooze button, don't lay your head back on the pillow for 10 minutes of so-called "sleep." Instead, sit up and close your eyes, take deep breaths, and focus on positive thoughts or nothing at all. If a concern or worry enters your mind simply acknowledge the thought and move on. Don't try to resolve any problems. Don't think about what you will do that day or the next. Don't do anything but relax and enjoy the peace and tranquility of the moment. A peaceful start to the day can change your entire perspective.

I try to begin each day positively, and this is one way I achieve that. Admittedly, it is a challenge to find a healthy balance between creating the life you desire, making time for loved-ones, and finding time to focus on self. I work more than 40 hours a week and am a part-time student. I am definitely not a list-maker, and my planner looks like a disaster zone. I have learned to be creative in developing time-managing techniques that fit well with my personality so that I will adhere to them. I've also reverted back to a lesson I learned before the age of two: there is nothing wrong with saying "No." After all, commitments we make to ourselves are just as significant as those we make to others. By allowing time for myself to pursue the simple things that create calmness in my life, I find I am more productive overall. When armed with a positive mentality and peace of mind, you have a greater power to create positive change in other areas of your life and the lives of those around you.

As a loving wife and a devoted mother, I enjoy spending quality time with my husband and child. However, just as important to me the time I spend with them is my own personal time. I remind myself everyday just how important I am to my family and to myself. After putting my child to bed and kissing my husband good night, I try to escape the realities of life by going to a little area in my house that I call my "special space." In this special place, I cuddle up with a good book, a cup of coffee, and unwind. While I'm in this space, I deflect all negative thoughts and reflect upon my day. During this period of reflection, I try to capture the lessons that I have learned. I also try to identify solutions to the dilemmas that I have been confronted with hoping to have the chance to put my plan into action the next day. Only when I am in my "special space" do I really realize how blessed I am. Sometimes the rigor of a day can block our view of the blessings we receive. Quiescence can allow us to appreciate our lives, along with helping us to find our place in the world. As a loving wife, I encourage my husband to find his own personal time as well. He too needs to be able to relax and unwind when he comes home from a busy day. This sometimes means that I purposefully try to avoid interrupting him while he's watching the "big game" because I realize that he too needs his self-time. As a mother, I teach my child the importance of self-time by helping him to appreciate his positive attributes and by encouraging him to participate in self-activities that hone his critical thinking skills. As a result, he has become a very talented artist and a great reader. As mothers, wives, and working professional women, we deserve quiescence. As women, we need to recognize the role that quiescence plays in our lives. When we begin to enjoy ourselves, others will begin to enjoy our company, and we can begin enjoying life!

REJECTION

"Rejection should not be a discouraging experience that will negatively affect a person's self-confidence or self-worth."

"Being rejected is never a measure of inadequacy, but it is instead a measure of your resilience."

In general, I think I deal with rejection in the same manner that most people do. I dwell on the whys and how comes for a brief period and then move on. However, I have not been able to apply that same philosophy to one area of my life, the feeling of rejection from my father. He has never openly rejected me, but his actions were daggers of rejection that left deep wounds.

Of course my father would never think of his life actions as rejection but that is what it has always felt like to me. I have always felt thrown away or discarded by my father. Time and time again, he chose his own selfish interests over the wants and most importantly the needs of his children. The thing that I still don't understand and will probably never understand is how you reject your own flesh and blood, especially babies and small children who are completely dependent upon their parents.

My father's rejection negatively affected me as a child, teenager, and still has lingering affects. As a small child and teenager I suffered from low self-esteem, which I camouflaged with an indifferent attitude. I also realize that as a young adult and possibly to this day some of my difficulties in relationships are the result of my relationship with my father. It's amazing that I even care about my father's rejection because I really don't believe that my life would have been better with him around. Over the years, prayer has helped me release some of the anger I feel towards him, but every now and then some of those feelings resurface. As long as I can remember, people have always talked about the importance of the father-son relationship, but my experiences have taught me that the relationship between a father and his daughter is equally as important, if not more.

I react to rejection in different ways depending on the situation. In the case of personal rejection, I usually seek the support of others. Prayer has also been an essential means of helping me gain a positive perspective of the circumstance. If the rejection involves a person, I may simply choose to eliminate the stress by disassociating myself from the person or situation. In my professional life, I usually am not bothered if my idea or suggestion is rejected. I instead try to keep an open mind to my colleagues' and learn from their constructive criticism. During childhood, rejection in any manner affected my self-esteem and self-confidence. Rejection, in any manner, can cause you to doubt yourself and react negatively. After dealing with various life experiences and becoming more mature, I don't react the same way to rejection as I did when I was younger. I still can have my "pity party," but it usually does not occur for a long period of time. In personal relationships, rejecting others has been difficult because it is hard for me to be polite and respectful if I feel hurt about the situation that led to the rejection. I was brought up to treat others the same way I wish to be treated. I am aware of how I have behaved in situations where I have rejected someone else. Many times, my reactions to these situations should have been handled differently. I now have made a conscious decision to learn from my past mistakes and avoid repeating the same behaviors that were once viewed as rude and negative. I have rejected friends for one reason or another and some of the friendships did not end on good terms. I did not behave in a polite manner and did not care at the time. Honesty is usually the best policy when rejecting someone. People are more likely to respond in a positive manner when they receive rejection that is free of negativity and harsh undertones. Rejection should be a learning experience that encourages an individual to grow from his or her actions. It should also motivate a person to modify his or her behavior to ensure a better outcome in the future. Rejection should not be a discouraging experience that will negatively affect a person's self-confidence or self-worth. Learning the proper ways, in which to reject a person can ultimately result in an encounter that is positive and enlightening for all involved parties.

Being rejected is never a measure of inadequacy, but it is instead a measure of your resilience. Throughout my lifetime, I have been faced with many situations in which rejection played a starring role. From relationships to career opportunities, I have encountered rejection on personal and professional levels. Until my high school years, I always took rejection personally; thereby inducing more scrutiny on myself, particularly my self-worth, self-confidence, and self-efficacy. However, after actualizing that what people said to me or thought of me really had no serious barring on who I was, I began to think and feel better about the act of rejection. As a result, I placed less weight on the act of being rejected. I instead began to utilize rejection as a self-learning tool.

It was so interesting to me that the opinions others had of me vastly differed from how I felt about myself. Using rejection as a motivator, I often approached it in a competitive manner. For some reason, I found great satisfaction in "winning over" an individual who had once rejected me, especially in intimate relationships. In fact, this strategy became a reality for me in dating. In almost 100 percent of the cases, in which I had been rejected by a male companion, was I later able to win him over. Unfortunately, after "winning" the guy over, my mission was accomplished and I in turn became the "rejector." While this manner of dealing with rejection may seem asinine, the lesson it can teach is quite simple—that no situation of rejection is definite. While one day a woman may be a victim, the next day she may emerge as the conqueror. I still hold strong these values, especially to those who have rejected me without due reason. All in due time, I am confident that they will regret not giving me a chance, whether personally or professionally.

I despise being rejected, especially when I am unsure of the rationale behind the rejection. In many cases when an individual rejects someone he or she never bothers to share with the "rejected" what could have been done in order to avoid the rejection. Offering constructive criticism to someone you are rejecting is a great way to help that person avoid being in the rejection seat in the future. Why do so many people feel rejection has to be an impersonal experience? Rejection should award the one who is being rejected an opportunity to learn from his or her mistakes. Being harsh and cruel while rejecting someone is not only counterproductive, but also inhumane.

I will never forget the day I realized that our friendship was over. The cold and empty look that you gave me as you waved goodbye should have been an indication that all was not well, but I ignored the warning. I felt the disconnection, I felt the emptiness, and I felt the rejection. Years passed before I could fully understand why you had rejected our friendship. It became evident that you weren't rejecting me, you were rejecting the successful woman I had become. Looking at me gave you a mirror image of all the successes you could have had, but did not achieve. This experience taught me the disheartening reality of how inevitable rejection is in our lives. Many times we spend years investing our time into building solid relationships only to have them deleted from our mental hard drives within a blink of an eye and without understanding the reason behind their departure. I have learned my lesson well—to guard my heart and understand the unpredictable nature of human beings. On our lonely walk down the road of disappointment, our eyes can be opened wide to the many opportunities that life has to offer us. Although this relationship truncated abruptly, I am happy to have learned so many lessons from it about the acceptance of rejection. Don't allow your self-perception to become affected by rejection. There are times when you will be rejected by others because of your ambitions or achievements. Be alert and recognize when others are rejecting you because of their own personal issues. Don't ponder over their insecurities. Keep your head up and continue moving towards your goal.

I have experienced a few instances of rejection with female friends. In most cases, these situations were more painful than being rejected by men because I felt we had established a higher level of camaraderie, trust, and expectations. As a result of the value that I place in my relationships, dealing with any type of rejection is difficult. However, it becomes even more difficult when individuals who reject you try to persuade others to do the same. After being rejected, I would always attempt to conduct candid discussions with the involved parties regarding why the rejection occurred. Some of the times the feedback that was shared was eye-opening and other times it was non-existent. I used to dwell on the reasons behind the rejection, but now I learn from it what I can and move forward. The feeling of rejection can conjure thoughts of failure and loneliness. However, we must suppress those negative thoughts and work to heal the hurt. Even when I felt I had been unfairly wronged or rejected, I realized I had to forgive, so I could heal the hurt that I was experiencing and take away from it the lesson I was meant to receive. After rejection or betrayal, it's difficult to trust again, but in order to heal we must forgive and move on. As a result, we will become stronger, better, and wiser! In some cases, the rejection could be a blessing in disguise!

SACRIFICE

"Sacrifice is a commitment that should be looked upon as temporary rather than permanent."

"Sacrifice is ultimately about defraying your own personal interests because the interests of others need to be considered first."

Usually when people use the word sacrifice they use it in a negative connotation. However, sacrifice can be a good thing. When I think of sacrifice, I begin to think of the sacrifice a mother makes to give love and time to her child. Of course, many people believe that they are making materialistic sacrifices for their children. However, the birth of a child should be viewed as a blessing, not a sacrifice. When I embark on parenthood myself, perhaps my view will change. Thus far, I have been blessed to feel that providing for my child is my responsibility, not a burden.

When one makes a sacrifice to obtain success or accomplish a goal, it pays off in the long run. In my career, I have sacrificed continuing my education to take a career advancement opportunity. Thus far it has paid off and has given me a chance to think about the direction I would like to take. When I decide to resume continuing my education, I will have to make the necessary sacrifices in my schedule and leisure time. Perhaps, this change will also cause a financial sacrifice for my family. One major part of sacrifice is being able to see the big picture as you embark on a goal. Sacrifice is a commitment that should be looked upon as temporary rather than permanent.

Sometimes sacrifice involves relinquishing the hold you may have on the happiness another can achieve. While in college, I sacrificed a relationship with the perfect gentleman because my focus was more on exploring life and less geared towards dating. Although this decision devastated me, I realized that not making this sacrifice would have hindered me from reaching my full potential as a woman. I also knew the personal quest I sought would deem me incapable of giving him the love and devotion he truly deserved. Needless to say, I soon found out that my sacrifice was another woman's gain. While I was trying to find my identity, another woman's love found him. Yes, I admit I was initially hurt by the discovery, but at the same time I was happy for him because I knew he was happy. The lesson here is very simple—when you make a sacrifice you must be informed of the risks involved. You must also thoroughly examine the consequences and determine whether the risk is worth the loss. Sacrifice means we must demolish our own selfish desires to address the needs of others we care about. On the upside of this experience, I was awarded a number of opportunities—the opportunity to learn an invaluable life lesson, discover my identity, and develop into the confident, self-assured, and content woman I am today.

I have made many sacrifices to meet the needs and demands of others in my personal and professional life. For the past eight years, I have made immense sacrifices by pursuing a career in the human services industry. My line of work has drained my time and mental energy so much that I have often contemplated leaving my profession. It's amazing that taking on such a massive job responsibility can translate into numerous personal sacrifices. So much of my time had been spent trying to help others that I have had very little time to deal with my own issues. At times, I feel like screaming, crying, and pulling out my hair, but I know I have to keep it all together. I realize that sacrifice is about doing things that you sometimes despise just because you know the job has to be done. At the age of 30, one of the most difficult sacrifices I have made was putting my career goal over having a family. In order for me to progress professionally, I know I have to sacrifice performing certain duties to maintain employment and continue to be promoted. I try to assist others the best way I can, and change my selfish behaviors. I always try to make the necessary changes or deal with life's stressors in an effort to live a productive and meaningful life. Sacrifice is ultimately about defraying your own personal interests because the interests of others need to be considered first.

I can't truly say that I've had to sacrifice much to be where I am today. I've worked extremely hard, but it doesn't classify as sacrifice. There is a distinction between working hard and sacrifice. When I think of sacrifice, I think of my mother. I think of the times she would go without to ensure that her children had whatever they needed. I think of the fact that my brother and I owned cars before she owned one. I think of the fact that she has never had a house to call her own, yet I have owned two. Many of my accomplishments would not have been possible without the love and selflessness of my mother. She sacrificed many of her dreams and aspirations to enable her children the opportunity to pursue their own dreams and goals. To many people this is what any parent would do, but life has taught me differently. In today's society, I think there are very few people who would sacrifice everything for another human being, even for their own children. I thank God for the sacrifices my mother made on my behalf. I also pray that when situations arise, in which I will need to make sacrifices, I will have half of her strength.

In my quest to become a successful woman, I have made many sacrifices. Many of these sacrifices have allowed me the chance to excel professionally, while others have caused me to forego opportunities. As most success stories have a price to pay, my price is the cost of sacrificing my liberation for parenthood. To me the idea of motherhood has always been just that, an idea. While I am excited about the joys that motherhood could deliver into my life, I am afraid that this eternal commitment will stifle my freedom. I know a number of women in my age group who are anxiously watching their biological clocks tick, but while they monitor their clocks, I am cherishing the last few free moments that I have. I admit to bearing selfish ideals about motherhood and the sacrifices involved, but I know when the time comes I will bungee jump into infinite responsibilities and the joys that await me. Sacrifices can teach us a great deal about our patience and lack thereof. Only God knows what we need and when we need it. When we wait and allow him to guide our steps, the results can be grand. Yes, motherhood will bring about new changes, but I think these changes will be well worth the sacrifice.

TRUANCY

"When the time is right, I too will be able to experience the happiness of knowing that the voids in my life no longer exist."

"It is no doubt that our lives will be filled with voids. However, most important in sustaining your mental wellness, is how you combat these losses and turn them into positive experiences."

I always have a man in my life. Whenever one relationship ends, I find a new man to fill the void that was left by the last. Usually the new one has a quality I deemed the other one to be lacking. If one is too goody-goody, the next one will be rebellious. If I date someone who is exceedingly aloof, I'll seek out someone attentive to replace him. If I don't meet anyone, that's okay too; I have male friends that can fill in as temporary boyfriends. Is this based on some deep-seeded emotional issue? Hmmmm … I grew up surrounded by a loving family, I have a good relationship with my father, and I don't have a fear of abandonment. My problem is simply that I don't know what I want and don't want to be alone while I try to figure it out.

Unfortunately, there are disadvantages to jumping from one relationship to another. I usually seem to go to extremes in my relationships instead of finding a happy medium. I suppose I can finally conclude my rebound approach has been proven unsuccessful, since I have yet to meet that person whom I feel can give me all that I desire. I've been replacing single missing pieces of the puzzle, instead of considering all the elements involved in finding the relationship that's best for me. While I'm investing my time with Mr. Rebound, I might be missing out on Mr. Right (or at least Mr. As Right As Humanly Possible). I've decided to make a list of the qualities I want in a partner, and I've identified the type of relationship that I want. I'm going to use this as a guideline for my future relationships. If I meet someone and don't feel he possesses most of the qualities I'm looking for, then I'll try a new approach: staying single.

When applied to my life, truancy has meant periods when I was in limbo. There have been many times when I wasn't sure where I wanted to go or where I should be. There have been times in my life when I was present physically, but absent in mind. During my freshman year in college, I experienced serious burnout over playing basketball, but I felt as if I couldn't just stop … there were others really depending on me. I often felt as if my cup was half full because I didn't know who I was or what I wanted. Now in retrospect, I look at those times as blessings. It is because of these experiences that I have been able to dabble into many different career fields. What's even funnier is that the one career field that I have always been called to is the same one I have finally decided to pursue at the age of 32. There's never a way to predict what will occur in our lives.

I have found an interesting way to cope with the presence of voids in my life—by avoiding them. My belief is that if I can just ignore the dilemma, then it will eventually play itself out, no matter what the outcome. I refer to this process of avoidance as APPLIED ATTENTION DEFICIT DISORDER. Whenever it is beneficial to me, I can give the matter at hand very limited attention if necessary.

Older and wiser, I now try to fill voids by seeking guidance from friends and prayer. If there is a decision I can't reach on my own, I seek refuge from others. I speak to my best friend almost several times a day, despite the fact that we are thousands of miles apart. With her help, problems seem to crumble and my voids seem to be filled.

Recently, I have experienced the lost of intimacy with a very close friend. I feel as if she is no longer the person I thought she was. I even question who she is period. To me, losing my personal connection with this friend has been quite devastating. Dealing with this loss has taught me a valuable lesson and has caused me to reexamine the truancy issues that I possess.

In order to address areas in my life, which I consider to be truant, I find positive ways to cope. Most effective for me are prayer, listening to inspirational music, and meditating. I have experienced losing both someone and something. No matter what the reason for the loss, I go through an intense grieving process. Sometimes, I become numb or go into a mild state of shock. Once this occurs, it is difficult for me to focus and actualize the circumstance. If the loss was due to death, the reality doesn't sink in until during the funeral. As a matter of fact, I sometimes avoid funerals just to delay the reality of dealing with the death. It is no doubt that our lives will be filled with voids. However, most important in sustaining your mental wellness, is how you combat these losses and turn them into positive experiences. There are numerous healthy ways to confront your issues with truancy, including gaining support from friends and family, exercising, participating in positive activities, and most effective of them all—prayer.

The area of my life that I feel is the most unfulfilled is my professional life. In my current job position, I don't feel like I am fully able to reach my potential. I am in a confined position that has the potential to be rewarding, but isn't satisfying to me. I am looking for something that is more flexible and will enable me to become more independent. I believe my purpose in this world is far beyond anything I am doing now. Therefore, I am focusing on my life, in particular, the goals that I want to accomplish. Although I am not currently involved in an intimate relationship, I do not feel unfulfilled in this area. However, I always embrace the possibility of meeting someone special.

I do sometimes feel a void in my "family life." At the holidays, especially Christmas and Thanksgiving, I experience a sense of loneliness and sadness because I do not feel attached to my family unit. My mother has converted to a religion that doesn't celebrate the holidays and has remarried. My sister is married with two kids and my father is deceased. I try to focus on the reason for the holidays and what it really means to me. On the brighter side, voids can sometimes motivate one to pursue his or her dreams. In this case, my sense of disconnection with my family members during the holidays, motivates me to one day have my own family. When the time is right, I too will be able to experience the happiness of knowing that the voids in my life have been filled.

While I would love to pretend that there are very few areas in my life that are truant, I confess with hesitation that this is not the case. My truancy issues are related to my inability to bear children. I am reminded of this inadequacy every time I hold a friend's baby or see a family with children. I want so badly to experience motherhood, but don't foresee the possibility of doing so. I know that this is one void I may never be able to fill, but have faith that God will eventually provide a solution. I have prayed about my circumstance and realize that I don't have to bear children biologically in order to erase this mark of truancy. I guess all that matters is that I am able to give love to a child who is in need of it. After all, this is the true meaning of motherhood. As I strive to obtain a life that is fulfilled, I try to remain patient and open-minded. I also try to avoid overshadowing God's plan. When we realize who is in charge, we can rest assured that the answers to our problems will be resolved and that all will be well and truancy-free.

There was a time in my life when shopping healed all wounds. If I broke up with a guy, I went shopping. If I had a bad day at work, I went shopping. I woke up to shop, got wireless internet to shop and had over 10 credit cards to do what? SHOP! Shopping filled many voids until the unhealthy habit turned into unhealthy debt. I didn't want to answer the phone because I feared it was a bill collector. I didn't want to go to the mailbox because there were so many bills. As I got older, wiser and more financially savvy, I learned to fill my voids in healthier, more productive ways. I started working out, began meditating, and found peace through prayer. Praying allowed me to develop a relationship with a higher power. This relationship has helped me fill my voids by enabling me to develop higher self-esteem, a more positive self-concept, and a happiness that only comes from within.

UMBRAGE

"Hate of any kind makes you feel less than a person."

"When you free yourself from umbrage, you are empowering your mind to think and communicate clearly."

Make no mistake about it. I am a grudge holder, but not out of malice. I simply don't like to be mistreated or taken advantage of. I really try to give 100% to others and wish for them to do the same. Sometimes, I think I am too nice and over the years, I have become more jaded and less forgiving of others who take advantage of my kindness. There are just some things that I won't and can't tolerate in relationships, e.g. lying, cheating, stealing, and dishonesty. Whenever, I encounter such an action, I immediately delete that person's name from my friendship list. It seems, the older I have become, the more I hold grudges. Only recently have I been able to release my hurtful actions over to God. This has helped me deal with the hatred and feelings of malice that I sometimes experience. It has also enabled me to feel better in mind and spirit. When you free yourself from umbrage, you are empowering your mind to think and communicate clearly. In many cases, once I have calmed down my emotions, I realize that the situation was all just a big misunderstanding that got out of hand because I was overcome by umbrage. In order to move forward with prosperity, we must avoid harboring bitterness and animosity.

As a child, I recall saying "I hate you" or "I hate something," but I had absolutely no idea how powerful these words were. Although, the statement was intended to make the person feel bad, my intentions were to inflict upon them temporary not permanent pain. Unfortunately, sometimes our hateful words are hurtful as well. When we become upset, we are so relentless with our expressions that we fail to think about the impact these words can have on an individual. While I cannot deny ever being upset or having feelings of resentment towards someone, I can say that most of the unhappiness or displeasure I have experienced has not resulted in hatred. In fact, I cannot recall ever being in a situation with someone who left me bitter or hating an entire population. Whatever situation you may encounter, it is your responsibility to channel your joys and sorrows. Personally, my religion and spirituality are driving forces for hindering umbrage from being a part of my life.

I attempt to see the good in all people, but sometimes my judgment is clouded by my past experiences. As I reflect upon my childhood experiences, I remember times in which I became the prey for many of my peers. On occasions, I was teased, taunted, and became the punch line in many jokes. At the time, I didn't know how to deal with those situations. I was ridiculed for no reason, so I fought back. Now, I realize that the anger and self-resentment issues my peers had were an indication of their insecurities. They were not able to appreciate the good in me because they questioned their own self-worth.

Hatred has come to me in many different forms. Many times I had no idea that the HATE even existed until it was too late. It is imperative that we all deal with our issues of hatred. Allowing these negative feelings to fester, will only be detrimental to the wellness of our minds, bodies, and spirits. Hate of any kind makes you feel less than a person. Through reading the Bible and attending church classes, I've learned that I should not hold hate and hostility in my heart. Instead, I should include God in all aspects of my life. Henceforth, I pledge to love everyone no matter what and combat umbrage with the shining armor that God has given me.

Today, I decided to clean out my closet. I'm not referring to the clothes closet in my bedroom, but the closet in my heart. After years of holding others accountable for my downfalls, I've decided that I'm in need of a serious emotional makeover. However, this makeover will not involve a third party advising me on how I need to overcome my internal conflicts. This makeover will instead be orchestrated by the only person who can truly relate to my most inner feelings—me. I have decided that a major renovation is necessary in order for me to move forward with a life that is free of bitterness and resentment towards others. With an attitude adjustment on the horizon, I plan to begin my cleaning regimen by vacuuming out the malicious thoughts I have of others when their successes outweigh mine, dusting out the bitterness that resides in my heart because I'm more than 30 years old and still unmarried, and mopping out the old flames of hostility that burn within my soul when I think of those friends turned foes that have betrayed and deceived me time after time. I've carried this torch of umbrage for decades and it is now time that I extinguish this flame.

How do we get past our hurts and wish our enemies well? What happens when the enemy is your husband? Boyfriend? Life partner? There are times when it is hard to witness people do well when they have hurt you or your family in some way. It is not easy to see past the pain and leave the person's accountability in the hands of a higher power. We must learn to look deep down inside ourselves to focus on the great things that we possess. We can't dwell on the hurt and pain we once felt because it only blocks the good things that are left to come. It is imperative that we learn from our mistakes and free ourselves from the injustices of pain. It takes a strong person to realize that life's obstacles serve as life's lessons. Marriage teaches you about love. Break-ups teach you about dating. Divorce teaches you about forgiveness. Pain teaches you about life.

VITALITY

"A strong mind and spirit are the foundation of a healthy lifestyle."

"Our inner spirits reside in a humble place that only has room for very few tenants.
One of these tenants is vitality."

Vitality is what keeps you going. It makes you want to get up in the morning and face the day. Vitality is infused in mental, intellectual, social, physical and spiritual wellness. The mind controls vitality. If you say you feel good, your body will follow. Don't let your mouth speak anything that your mind or body is not prepared to handle. Mental vitality makes all of the other components fall into line and operate at top speeds. People sometimes underestimate the power we have in our minds. A strong mind and spirit are the foundation of a healthy lifestyle. I maintain my own vitality by setting attainable goals, praying, and maintaining a relationship with God. For I know that through him, my vitality will be everlasting.

My belief is that the essence of life can be found only through our intrinsic components. Our inner spirits reside in a humble place that only has room for very few tenants. One of these tenants is vitality. Vitality is the warm and energetic spirit that cannot be fueled by medication or vitamins. It is essential to the soul, but most importantly all facets of wellness. Vitality is a prescription that never needs to be refilled. I have seen my mother exude this energy. In her early sixties, she is just as vibrant and energetic as she was 30 years ago. She exercises daily, eats rights, and maintains her spirituality through reading the Bible. I can only pray to assume the vitality that she exemplifies when I become her age. My energy emerges from my joy of life. This energy is a natural high.

Vitality and energy are synonymous to me. Vitality *is* the energy to live. Vitality is the energy to get up each morning, to seek and acquire knowledge, to pursue happiness, to express emotion, to welcome all that life has to offer. Vitality encompasses all parts of being—physicality, mentality, and spirituality. Just recently, the physical aspects of vitality came into greater focus for me when my physician ordered that I have a biopsy. This is the first time in my life that I have considered the possibility of having a serious illness. At the same time, I was dealing with migraine headaches, which can be almost debilitating at their worst. I pride myself on being a healthy person, so being faced with illness and dealing with uncontrollable headaches felt like a sign of weakness. I was disappointed that I could not control the pain and "just get over it." Being sick made me feel like a failure, although I know I should not have thought this way. After getting over my initial unease, I decided to make a more serious commitment to strive for total vitality. I know there are some things that cannot be avoided, but I intend to do what I can to maintain a healthy body. I've gained an increased appreciation for the fact that this is the only body I have and I want to treat it with the utmost care.

I often wonder how women live their lives without vitality and still experience happiness. Life is too short not to experience the vigor that life has to offer. On a daily basis we encounter experiences that allow us to see how blessed we are, but yet we allow ourselves to focus on the negative aspects of life. If you know that no day is promised to you, why would you ever allow yourself to walk out of the house each morning with a spirit that lacks vitality? Each day you commit this act, you are showing God that you don't appreciate the day He has given you. You must begin to appreciate your life, but first you must begin to appreciate yourself. Doing so will help you appreciate living your life. Only then will you be able to experience vitality.

After a long day at work, I find it very difficult to find vitality at home unless it's in my bed. By the time I arrive at home, fix dinner for my husband and child, I don't have an ounce of energy left; my fuel level is low. It amazes me when I see other mothers who work full-time jobs just as I do, with so much vitality. I cannot imagine how these women can conjure up enough energy to perform their parental duties and still be attentive to their other responsibilities. I guess I need to spend more time focusing on my blessings and not the hassles of a day. Maybe then I'll be able to experience vitality as well.

Vitality is energy. Vitality is mental. It's that "uumph" that you rely on to get going. I think my gas tank is on "E." I have truly lost some of my vitality. I think that motherhood has changed me in ways that I would have never imagined. Prior to having kids, I had vitality. Sometimes the addition of life changes means your priorities will change as well—and not always for the better. It is hard for some of us to maintain vitality. Maintaining vitality is just one more "thing to do" to add to our long list of "things to do." Sometimes in the grand scheme of things, we eliminate things that we think can wait or seem unimportant at the time. We, especially as women, will put others first and ourselves last. We should never forget about ourselves. It's a challenge to find the right balance, but it is necessary. Recently, I started working out and can actually feel the difference; my vitality is coming back. Life seems to flow just a little better with vitality. I feel like I can keep up in the race of life and not get run over. Can life be "productive" without vitality? Maybe so, but I do believe life is so much better with it.

WOMANHOOD

"As an adult, I embrace all of the aspects of womanhood that once petrified me."

"Being a woman means power. The power to influence, encourage and support."

I walked down the tan hallways lined with bright yellow lockers. The bell had sounded 5 minutes ago, so I was late and the halls were empty. I saw a fellow classmate, my friend, walking from the other end of the building. As we closed in on the door to our Algebra I classroom, I greeted my classmate with a gracious hello. He responded by reaching out and placing his hands on my chest. I felt ashamed, embarrassed, and confused. As I stood there with my mouth hanging open, he casually walked on as though he'd responded to my greeting accordingly. I was furious. Sadly, I admit to experiencing several incidents like this as a young woman: from having someone attempt to force himself on me sexually, to a college professor implying my work-study with him was dependent upon obliging him with a date. I used to feel so baffled by these advances. Was this what being a woman is all about? Does having breasts and a vagina signify an open invitation for harassment? Is a woman defined by her sexuality? When I was a younger woman I felt powerless. I know that this instance isn't an example of the behavior exemplified by all men; just a few bad apples. Now as an older and more experienced woman, I feel empowered. I know that being a woman doesn't have anything to do with someone's unwanted advances or lewd remarks. I know how to express to a man that his behavior is inappropriate and that I don't have to accept it. I know that my womanhood is defined by so much more than my sexuality, but that it is okay to be comfortable with my sexuality. Yes, I admit it ... I'm sexy!

Being a woman means power—the power to influence, encourage and support. Being a woman means love—being able to give love even if it means not getting it in return. Being a woman means responsibility—having the responsibility of birthing and caring for others. For me, being a woman means being a living legacy. A legacy for sons and daughters to admire, encompassing all virtues. My femininity is a power. I have the ability to bless you or manipulate you with it. It allows me to be equally yoked with my masculine counterparts when necessary. The actual power lies in knowing when to use your masculine and feminine qualities. I believe that men and women view life differently because of the many experiences that we have had and how we were raised. The commonalties are the goals that we have for ourselves and our families. We may choose different roads, but our journeys will lead us to experiences that will develop our legacies. Some people may view assertive women as masculine due to their own definitions, experiences or lack thereof. It is an oddity for a woman to be "straight forward" or "tough-skinned" because men have been termed with these characteristics. In the workplace, to be assertive is a valued asset. It is important not to be scrutinized as weak or irresolute. Women who are assertive in the workplace are valued and respected.

Other women contribute to your growth into womanhood. Whether it is positive or negative, you determine if you will emulate or discount their attitudes. Fortunately, I grew up with numerous strong positive women role models. All of these women exemplified a variety of attributes. I watched these women effectively use their intellect and quick wit to get what they wanted out of life, from money to men. I admired my grandmother's ability to be humble and meek, my aunt's ability to entertain and be creative, and my mother's independence. The ladies in my family loved hard and valued their own individualism and morals. When I reflect upon these women, I think of the compassion and nurturing qualities that they possessed. These qualities have helped me to become the positive, self-sufficient, and confident woman that I am today and I thank them for instilling in me strong values of love, integrity, and pride. I can only surmise that my legacy will encourage women to pursue their dreams while enjoying womanhood. Womanhood is a journey, in which we will gather thoughts and ideas that will shape us into *virtuous* people, physically and cognitively. Our legacies do not have to be created when we are old, preparing for death, or recording life stories! Everyday is an opportunity to establish a legacy. What will your legacy as a woman be?

Womanhood is by far one of the most exhilarating experiences one could ever experience. Sexy one minute, then feisty and demanding the next—who could ask for any more dramatic a transformation? In my earlier years, I simply equated the concept of womanhood with endless make up sessions, the onset of menstruation, and wearing brassieres. I associated womanhood with responsibility and infinite commitments to household duties, none of which captured my interest. In fact, it took me more than 15 years to even realize that being a woman had so many privileges. I am now cognizant that being a woman is so much more than being dainty, prissy, and feminine all of the time. It means that you can exemplify these attributes, while still "kicking butt" professionally and personally. As an adult, I embrace all of the aspects of womanhood that once petrified me. It's amazing how a difference of years can bring about such drastic and positive changes. The key to this change however, is accepting the role that God has destined for you. Whether it is in your interest to bear children or pursue marriage, you must first realize your purpose. My mission is to enjoy life as a woman to the fullest and pro-voke positive change in women all around me, young and old.

Sometimes I despise being a woman. Aside from my annoyance with feminine experiences like menstrual cycles, bloating, and yeast infec-tions, I also despise the gender roles that society places on women. These roles such as cooking and cleaning only add to the stack of responsibilities that women already assume including working full-time jobs and taking care of children. Most of my married friends are always complaining about their lazy husbands who do nothing at home, except add to their pile of household chores. I hope being a woman has more privileges than just being someone else's servant. I want to enjoy my womanhood. More than that, I want my womanhood to be enjoyed, appreciated, and not taken for granted.

X-RAY

"Performing an X-ray is essential to self-repair. In order to diagnose our personal issues, we must dig deep to assess our malfunctions."

"Always under a constant X-ray, I can't afford to do anything wrong, not even gain 5 pounds (sigh)."

There are times when I feel I am being X-rayed by others and that I am being unnecessarily critical of myself. As a result of my self-criticism, I am always trying to "perfect" some aspect of myself or become better using the characteristics I value as a guide. I feel that I am pretty open to criticism coming from others when it is constructive. However, in the past, I have felt unjustly criticized and blame has developed out of some ulterior motive. I feel hurt and disappointed when this happens in particular when I have exhibited the same behaviors seen in other people or friends and their actions are overlooked. Due to my experiences, I am trying to be less critical of myself. I am also trying to surround myself with people who value my friendship and are not trying to scrutinize me just because they think I will accept it.

In regards to my professional life, my self-criticism has become crippling to my career goals because I constantly over examine the projects or tasks, in which I am involved. I describe my behavior as crippling because it often precludes me from adhering to deadlines and occasionally causes me to miss opportunities. My critical nature results from being a zealous, industrious, and conscientious person. While having these qualities is usually an asset, I am learning that balancing my self-scrutiny is far more effective than allowing it to hinder my performance.

In my personal life, I believe my kindness and sincerity is sometimes taken for a weakness and on two occasions have become the object of scrutiny from "so called" college friends who found comfort in being critical of me. In the past, I have taken an honest assessment of myself and tried to examine what I could do to improve these traits. Performing an X-ray is essential to self-repair. In order to diagnose our personal issues, we must dig deep to assess our malfunctions. In some cases, we have to relinquish inhibitions and dissolve friendships that are not beneficial to our well-being. Through my experiences, I learned that just as I am under the X-ray by others, I must also take the necessary steps to conduct a thorough examination of those whom I wish to befriend. Our personal wellness is not only determined by our actions, but also by the actions of those who surround us.

As a 29 year old single woman, I feel like I'm always being X-rayed. In particular, my singlehood has become the crux of family discussions. When I see my old college friends, most of them seem to be either getting married, married, or once married. My family members only add to the dilemma by asking me "when are you getting married?" At times, this situation can become overwhelmingly stressful. Even in dating, I feel like I'm being X-rayed. Almost immediately after the introduction, the man begins sizing me up to see if I am "good" enough to be his wife. At the same time he's evaluating me, he's not considering if he even meets my expectations for a husband. This is definitely a major turn off for me. On top of that, it's frustrating! Although I am proud of my accomplishments, my success at this point has become a target for criticism. It seems that everything I do will cause people to pull out their magnifying glass only to become critical of me. Sometimes the high expectations one develops for you can be hindering to your personal freedom. Always under a constant X-ray, I can't afford to do anything wrong, not even gain five pounds (sigh).

At 28, I am comfortable with who I am. I have reached a point where I am not ashamed of my weaknesses or imperfections. I acknowledge them and am working on those things I feel I need to change. Overall, I am very happy with who I am, but feel I must constantly work towards being an even better person. One of my greatest struggles has been to allow myself to be vulnerable to others. I rarely outwardly express emotions such as fear or grief, even to family or close friends. When I face a daunting obstacle, I rarely let anyone know. I don't want to speak negatively or be a burden to others, and I therefore isolate myself emotionally. Over time I have learned to let down my guard. I do feel that internal strength is a wonderful quality to posses; however I also know there are times when I could benefit from seeking the support of those close to me. I also realize that if I want my relationships to continue to grow, I will have to be willing to give more of myself.

In the past, I have beaten myself up over what I perceived as a glaring flaw. Now I recognize that my "imperfections" are pieces of the puzzle that create my individuality. I have learned to be more accepting of myself. In reflection, accepting my flaws is what has actually helped me to open myself up to others. I feel an important key to acceptance is being able to differentiate between an imperfection and behavior that is destructive. I accept the fact that I prefer to deal with problems on my own, but recognize that if I feel overwhelmed or unable to find resolution it is okay to seek out someone's advice or comfort. I am most proud of the times I am able to influence or create positive change in someone's life.

When I witness someone undergoing struggles or in anguish I feel compelled to help if I have the means to do so. I strongly believe it is my moral responsibility to make a positive contribution to the society in which I live. I encourage anyone who doubts her significance in this world to do something selfless for a person in need. This person could be someone without shelter or sustenance, or this person could be a friend in need of a non-judgmental ear. When you see that you are able to provide a basic need, comfort or ease a person's mind you will recognize the powerful force you really have.

YOUTH

"Although, I have one more year before I turn the big "3-0," I have been reflecting upon my twenties and making some serious decisions to ensure that I can maintain the spirit of my youth."

"I am thankful for all of the life lessons that my youth has taught me and thankful for the woman that was created as a result."

Youth is like the succession of the sun, we wake each morning to learn and experience something new and shed light on the world around us just as the sun ascends each morning to illuminate a world that's a little different than it was the day before. It's all about the existence of future possibilities: When I was four, I couldn't wait for the upcoming year so that I could stretch out all five fingers of my little hand and declare, I'm five!? When I was 17, I gleefully anticipated experiencing my first taste of freedom in college. Now, with my 29th birthday fast approaching, there are never-ending rays of options and opportunities shining in front of me. I believe I will feel youthful as long as I have the desire to explore these possibilities. I don't worry about the fact that I am getting older, but I do fear losing the joys of being young. I wonder if I will lose my looks or my health. Will I feel like I'm running out of time to obtain all I desire? Will I be happy with the choices I'm making now? I could come up with countless questions to ponder over. In their place I try to think about how my mother would respond to these kinds of questions. Like many parents, she was sometimes ambushed with a barrage of "what if" scenarios: What if nobody likes me? What if I fail my test? What if something bad happens? On those occasions she would simply ask in return, Okay, now what if that doesn't happen??

I try to counteract my fears in the same way. After all, no one is handing out crystal balls with visions of the future. Each day will bring something unique with it, and fearing what is to come will only hold me back. So instead of fearing what might happen, I'll look forward to announcing I'm twenty-nine and optimistically welcome all that comes with it!

At this point in my life, I still don't feel like a grown woman, I feel like a young woman. The life experiences that I have acquired thus far cannot be equated to those of a mature woman. I also lack the wisdom that a mature woman possesses. When I was younger, I had minimal responsibilities. However, now as a single and independent woman, I have assumed a plethora of household duties, some inside and others out-side. It isn't rare to see me cutting my lawn, washing my car, or taking out the trash. I can't complain though, I rarely cook and live a pretty fancy-free life. I still however, reminisce about the days when I didn't have a care in the world, except making up my bed and performing a few household chores. I also miss taking summer vacations and staying home from school, even though this didn't happen very often. I believe getting older is an exciting thing. At times, I even wish I had the experi-ences of an older more seasoned woman. In my field of work, I do believe age makes a difference in the way my employees perceive me. When you are younger people will try to treat you in a different way, as if you are inexperienced.

No matter what your age, it is important that you are able to accept growing old. After all, nothing can be done to change your age, but everything can be done to alter the way your feel. Start now by appreci-ating the wisdom or naivety associated with your age. A confident and vivacious woman who is seventy years old will always maintain her youthful undertones as long as she feels that way. Contrarily, a young girl who acts three times her age will relinquish her youthful energy far too soon. I am coming to the end of my twenties and I have no problems telling people my age. Although, I have one more year before I turn the big "3-0," I have been reflecting upon my twenties and making some serious decisions to ensure that I can maintain the spirit of my youth. I never want to lose it!

Ah…. youth, the obsession of American culture (and me too). As my 30th birthday rapidly approaches, thoughts of my "younger days" are more and more frequent. What is it about turning 30, 40, or even 50 for that matter? Growing up, I always wanted to be older. Then I would be an adult and adults could do anything. Boy was I stupid! Now I want to slow down the clock, so I can enjoy my "youth." Who made the rule that says you are old at 30? I don't feel old. At times I feel like a woman.

Other times I find myself wishing I was still a young adult, and then I wouldn't feel so strange shopping in the juniors section of a department store. Although I am anxious about turning 30, I am also excited about what the next decade will bring and how long I can stretch shopping in the juniors' section. I'm looking forward to the wisdom that comes with age, but not the wrinkles.

Each year has brought a valuable learning experience and I'm sure 30 will be no different or any year after that. I can't turn back the hands of time, so I won't contemplate alternative outcomes of my life. I am thankful for all of the life lessons that my youth has taught me and thankful for the woman that was created as a result.

One morning I woke up and I was old. Where did the time go? It's hard to believe that I'm not as youthful as I once was. I'm a thirty-something year-old woman with the looks of a twenty-something year-old woman. It is scary sometimes to think about getting older. I reminisce on my younger days and how much fun I used to have; I was so carefree. Now, as an adult, I still have fun, but I have more responsibilities.

As a mother and a wife, I think I notice my youth slipping away more. I can't run around as much as I used to. I don't stay up as late as I used to either. I don't even eat as much or the same foods I used to eat when I was younger. As I watch my children grow older, I realize more and more that I am the adult—the caregiver, the nurturer. I am all of the things that I wasn't when I was a youth. Why is it that when you are younger, you want to be older and when you are older, you want to be younger? Although I enjoyed my younger days, I realize that one benefit to aging is the wisdom that is gained over the years. Even if I could stop myself from aging, I wouldn't. Youth is like the appetizer to a three course meal. It gives you a taste of what is to come!

ZENITH

"After years of wandering off of the road, I finally believe, I am on the path towards zenith, but it has not been without a great deal of assistance, hard work, frustration, anger, and faith that I will someday arrive."

"Your personal zenith is attainable, but cannot be reached until you develop personally."

In this fast paced and ever changing environment, I believe it is difficult to be satisfied with your current place in life for any extended period of time. As human beings we are always striving to reach the next plateau. In our constant state of change, our goals and desires are transforming and evolving as we discover and define our personal zenith. My experiences in life have shown me that my struggles are usually followed by a period of complete satisfaction and a sense of wholeness once I obtain my goals. Then the cycle starts over and before I realize it, I am struggling; exposed and vulnerable again, facing life's altering dilemmas. My moments of satisfaction are all too fleeting, but I know I will soon return to that point.

For young adults, I believe this struggle can be particularly challenging when faced with the onslaught of television shows and commercials, which try to convince viewers that reaching zenith involves medication, plastic surgery, or advice from a lifestyle guru. If this continues, we will be too medicated to separate reality from fiction. Sometimes I even find myself falling prey to products advertised on television and wondering if it is necessary in order to reach a point of complete utopia. Fortunately, reality returns and I quickly resolve that I can reach my "personal utopia" without any assistance from unnatural sources. Innately, I believe my "personal zenith" is attainable but I am unsure of how to obtain it. After years of wandering off of the road, I finally believe, I am on the path towards zenith, but it has not been without a great deal of assistance, hard work, frustration, anger, and faith that I will someday arrive.

In order to reach the zenith of our lives, we must set challenging, realistic and specific long-term goals. Once you follow through on what you've set for yourself, then you can chart your success. The most important aspects of my life right now are mostly related to self-development. It has nothing to do with career success, family, academics, economic empowerment or any of the main foci of America today. I am concerned about how I am maturing and growing spiritually, physically and mentally, who my friends are and how loyal I am to them. I am also concerned about the welfare of my family and how I can support them, instead of how they can support me. It is my goal to make sure that my behavior matches my values. I want to be known for my integrity, rather than my degrees or wealth. The successes that I have made are notable, but aren't what I would call necessary steps in order to get to the turning point. I do know that the turning point cannot happen until I master my own strengths. I am currently evolving, and once the evolution is complete, then my goals will be easier to attain. It is true that if you don't know where you are going, then you will not go anywhere.

I believe you will have many more turning points in your life. I can recall all of my points and all of them were not pleasurable. Listen up! All of your points will not be pleasurable. There will be times when you will think you have lost your mind.

I am not yet at the point of culmination, but I look forward to getting there. Neither am I satisfied with my current place in life, but I have had enough experience to know that it's fine to be achievement-oriented; perfection is impossible. We (ladies) often set super challenging goals with unrealistic time frames for ourselves. We are our worst enemies when these goals aren't reached.

Five years from now, I see myself revamping my goals for the next five years to follow. Alike our society, I am forever changing and growing. I envision myself as a smarter, stronger, and even more peaceful individual than I am now. As for my career and family, it is difficult to say. As far as my lifestyle, healthy, healthy, healthy is the forecast for my future. Your personal zenith is attainable, but cannot be reached until you develop personally. In order to get there I must begin with the end in mind—approaching my relationships with a win-win strategy and renewing myself periodically. This includes physical, mental, spiritual, and socio-emotional renewal. My last advice to you is that you begin to write out your goals and develop a personal mission statement. It is important to identify your strengths and weaknesses when developing your mission statement. Part of my mission is to lead a life that is centered on the principles of empowerment, honesty, integrity, and excellence. I realize that I must recognize my strengths and develop talents as a person who is clever, confident, generous, and optimistic. I must envision myself becoming a person who is fun, sensitive, wise, compassionate, opulent, and financially healthy. I must also emulate the admirable characteristics in others, such as being ambitious, compassionate, enthusiastic, creative, and educated. I must also attempt to implement similar characteristics in my own life. Lastly, I must place my focus on what truly makes me happy. To me, learning, relationships, family, happiness, and lifestyle are the elements of my zenith.

I have no concrete idea of what my *ultimate* goals are. I am ever-changing and with every change my perception of what is ideal is in someway altered. I look at these changes as life's lessons. They help me to understand what is most important to me, who I am, and who I wish to become. With each change—no matter how difficult—I can find delight in knowing that change is part of the progression towards my ideal self and my ideal life.

I sometimes feel pressure to have a "master plan." I feel like people expect me to know exactly what I want. It seems like many of my friends have a clear plan. They know where they want to live, know how many kids they want to have (if they don't already have them), and have defined clear career goals. They also seem to find success through following their carefully laid plans.

I, on the other hand, am utterly clueless at times! I consider myself a free-spirit; I hate to feel boxed-in or stuck to a particular path. I enjoy the excitement that comes from exploring different options. I think this aspect of my personality sometimes hinders me from setting stringent goals for myself. I don't have a desire to feel "settled" and I have not yet felt a great need for stability. However, I do understand that goals are an essential part of my life. Without them, all the ambition in the world will not lead to my success or the fulfillment of my life's purpose. There are several aspects of my ideal life that I juggle with in my mind. I think I should buy a house, but then hesitate because I don't know how long I wish to stay in this city. I can see my career possibly going in several very different directions, all of which hold equal appeal to me. And I recently stopped dating someone, so I have no idea who I may marry someday … and the thought of children seems very far off. It is sometimes scary to look forward and see such a fuzzy picture of the future. At the same time, it is exciting to contemplate what I might find as this picture becomes clearer. I believe every person must find their own way of creating realistic ways to attain their ideal life. For me, I think that setting short-term goals is the answer. I have outlined goals regarding finances, education, career and personal relationships. I've decided to focus on these aspirations within the next two years, and re-evaluate and re-define them if necessary. This way, I do not feel boxed in by endless plans, but I *am* actuating steps to build a positive future. I am focused on enjoying my current journey and trying to make the best decisions I can. I believe that if I do this, I will reach my zenith and it will be the right place for me.

Poetic Postlude
"A Glimpse at Life's Perspectives from A–Z"

Am-bi-tion, Beau-ty and **Cam-ar-aderie,**
Now that's only naming a few;
Try **Dating,** Good **Ethics** have **Faith,**
Examine **Glass Ceilings** and give **Homage** too.

We share **Inti-macy** right before **Jealousy,**
Some **Kindred** Spirits for all of your Souls;
With **Li-ber-ation, Money,** and **Naivety,**
Add a little **Op-ti-mi-sm** and you might strike Gold!

There's Per-ser-ver-ance and Quiescence,
We cope with **Re-jec-tion** perspective **R!**
We all **Sacrifice** and experience **Truancy;**
Still "Smashing Tomatoes" small or large!

We deal with **Umbrage** and V for **Vi-tal-ity,**
We share some lessons of **Womanhood;**
Then we **X-Ray** our **Youth** and the Z word **Zenith,**
From A to Z, yes it's all Good!

"At a Glance" we take a glimpse at life's Per-spec-tives,
All opinions are Candid, some are Real, and a few are Funny;
Just remember throughout this book journey,
That we didn't mean to "Smash your Tomatoes, Honey!"

© 2007 Written by Wanda D. Davis

EPILOGUE

"I DON'T MEAN TO SMASH YOUR TOMATOES, HONEY!

Acknowledging our weaknesses is not always an easy task. This process involves a great deal of self-reflection, self-analysis, and honesty. Sometimes it takes a friend or two to help us unveil and address those areas which are in desperate need of improvement. Coincidentally, the word tomato has historically been used as a colloquial expression to describe an attractive girl. Aside from this commonality, tomatoes and women share a number of other similar attributes. Both are versatile, can be naturally sweet, are good for the health of those that consume them, and are at their best when treated with care and allowed to ripen—to reach their full potential.

Similar to the tomato-a fruit that is often misperceived as a vegetable—women are often misperceived, misrepresented, and misunderstood. Yet, despite the challenges that some women encounter in their personal and professional lives, they remain an invaluable staple in many households and work environments around the world.

Just like a tomato, there are times when an occasional "pluck," "squeeze," or "smash" may be necessary in order for the essence of a woman's nectar to be released. Only when this "plucking," "squeezing," and "smashing" occurs will women truly be able to share their feelings and vent in a way that is healthy, gratifying, and meaningful. "Smashing

Tomatoes" with the people who are dearest to your heart will allow you to free yourself from your personal inhibitions and motivate you to open your box of possibilities. We hope you have found this book to be helpful in validating your opinions of life's perspectives and wish you the best in your journey towards success, joy, and prosperity both personal and professional.

About the Author

Dr. BerNadette Lawson-Williams currently resides in Charlotte, NC with her husband Don. She strongly advocates the necessity for women to maintain an open mind, open spirit, and open heart, so they can be open to the joys of life. Her hobbies include playing golf, skiing, dancing, and creative writing. BerNadette received her undergraduate degree from South Carolina State University, and graduate degrees from the University of Wisconsin-La Crosse and the United States Sports Academy. She is a member of Delta Sigma Theta Sorority, Incorporated and a native of Temple Hills, Maryland.

Tracie K. Thomas is a healthcare consultant and writer who resides in the Charlotte, NC area. Her educational goal is to complete a graduate degree in Public Health, so she can influence health policies and reduce disparities in healthcare that impact women, and other underserved populations. She feels her participation in this book project was an exercise of empowerment, and hopes to inspire other women to pursue their dreams. In her spare time she enjoys photography, decorating, and sharing laughs with family and friends.

978-0-595-43381-0
0-595-43381-2

LaVergne, TN USA
02 November 2009
162746LV00004B/176/A